Praying Through Paradox

One of the few professional social scientists who is also a theologian, Charles Elliott has lived in Africa and worked in Asia and Latin America. He has a deep respect for people at the bottom of the heap, especially in the rural areas, whence much of the material in this volume is gleaned.

He lives in inner-city London and mountain Wales, and is married, with three grown-up sons.

CHARLES ELLIOTT

Praying Through Paradox

Collins
FOUNT PAPERBACKS

First published in Great Britain in 1987
by Fount Paperbacks, London

Made and printed in Great Britain by
William Collins Sons & Co. Ltd, Glasgow

To those who live the paradoxes
this book is dedicated
in the ambitious hope that it will make it
a little easier

Acknowledgements

I am grateful to the BBC for allowing me to publish the text of six broadcasts from the series "Streams in the Desert", March 1986. The producer, Beverley McAinsh, helped improve the texts substantially, and I am accordingly grateful to her and her colleagues. My wife, Hilary, generously read the rest of the book in draft, and made many useful suggestions. I alone, however, am responsible for the remaining imperfections.

I acknowledge with appreciation the many letters I received as a result of the original broadcasts, and am humbled by the honesty with which many people shared their own stories.

Gwyneth Goodhead typed the manuscript with her usual efficiency and good humour. I am fortunate indeed in my secretarial assistant and acknowledge that thankfully.

Contents

We are the impostors who
   speak the truth,
the unknown men whom all men know;
dying we still live on;
disciplined by suffering, we are not
   done to death;
in our sorrows we have always
   cause for joy;
poor ourselves, we bring wealth to many;
penniless, we own the world.

2 Corinthians 6:8–10,
NEB

1.

Introduction

(i) About this book

This book started as six fifteen-minute broadcasts during Lent 1986. Following discussions with staff of the BBC's religious broadcasting department, I decided to include two features in the broadcasts which, though hardly revolutionary, might be thought a little unusual. The first was to use true stories as the main vehicle for developing the points I wanted to make. The second, closely related, was to encourage listeners to reflect on their own experience, their own story, during the broadcasts.

We are used, perhaps, to thinking of "history" as a way in which the Old Testament handles religious truth; and we are familiar with the "historical" story of Jesus' life and death in the gospels and of the spread of the Church in Acts. We know too the power of the fictional stories Jesus told, his parables, and modern scholars reinforce their power when they remind us that many of the parables were drawn from life.

Story is, therefore, a well-known way of communicating religious ideas, yet we tend to overlook the story element in the epistles. Often they seem turgid, dense, unattractive theological argumentation, scarcely related to the lives of ordinary people in the twentieth century. That there is some tough thinking and hard debating in Paul's letters is, of course, both true and important, yet behind the abstraction, there is the story of a man, a mission and two journeys, one geographical, one inward.

There are many ways of relating to that story. We can analyse it, intellectualize it, check it for consistency, for creativity, for authenticity. That is to relate to it with our minds. I do not want to be thought to be dismissive of that, not at all. A well-informed, reasoned appreciation of the subtleties of Paul's thought is the right of every Christian. Yet it often seems to me that if we seek to relate to Paul's story *only* at that intellectual level, we miss a large part of the point. The Bible as a whole is not, thank God, a theological textbook. It is a series of glimpses into the religious experience of individuals and communities, as they either undergo or reflect upon traumatic events that force them back to ultimate questions about their own identity and the nature of the world in which that identity is to be fashioned, expressed and redeemed.

I think this is a helpful way to read the epistles. To see them, that is, not as yawn-provoking theological treatises, but as glimpses of the process of the formation of religious consciousness. It is clear, for example, that the Pauline epistles (accepting the conventional ascriptions of authorship) do not present us with a neatly worked, coherent, logically ordered set of dogmas. Rather, what we have here – and no more so than in the letters to the Christians in Corinth – is theology-making-on-the-run. In writing them – more than the conventional two, as we shall see in a moment – Paul was reacting both to events around him and to his own experiences, experiences of rejection, criticism, failure and pain, as well as experiences of a deepening faith in a God of love who saves, sets free and brings joy to the whole of his Creation. His letters, then, are commentaries on the interaction – one might almost say interpenetration – of the flow of outward events and the counterflow of religious consciousness.

It is for that reason that I believe it is helpful if, alongside Paul's experiences – both "outer" and "inner" – we lay our own. The correspondence that the broadcasts evoked showed two things about this. First, it is uncharted territory for many people and therefore frightening, painful and "hard". Second, many (but not all) find it brings alive prayer — in its widest sense — in a way that correspondents described variously as "exciting", "shocking" and "amazing". These I suspect are extreme reactions, and I certainly would not expect most readers to find so highly-charged a response to the exercises and reflections in this book. Yet the truth, astonishing as it may seem in retrospect, is that we are not often encouraged to reflect on our experiences, our story, as though they are the stuff of divine revelation. We might expect to discern God in Scripture, in the lives of the great saints and, if we are lucky, in one or two extraordinarily holy people whom we are fortunate to meet during a life- time. The notion that God is *here* — in my life; today; in this wretched mess I have made of everything — is so wholly foreign to us that our prayers, divorced from where the action is, become oddly insulated from reality. If they then seem inauthentic, dry and finally dead or deadening . . . well, the acknowledgement of that is the faithfulness that makes progress possible.

I hope, then, that in reading this book, you will find the courage and the time to use the richness of your own story as a natural complement to the wealth of Paul's reflection on the interplay between faith and life. The temptation will be to read the chapter and promise yourself that you will come back to the hard bit — the exploration of your own feelings, memories and imagination: "I'll do it when I have time." "I'll read the whole book and then pick out the exercises that look helpful . . ." That is natural. We may need to ask, however, whether there is not also an element of defence about it. Exploring our past and our present is sometimes painful, for if we do it honestly — and there is no point in doing it at all unless we do it honestly — many of the comforting illusions with which we surround ourselves tend to be stripped away and we are left looking at ourselves as we really are.

That raises a crucial point, one that I want to emphasize with all the force I can command. Not one of the exercises here is an invitation to condemn yourself. Christ does not condemn us – ever. Even when the Jews brought him a woman caught in the very act of adultery, he told her – no doubt to her great surprise and the even greater surprise of her accusers – that he did not condemn her. He also told her to change radically the course of her life, but that is quite different. He refused to diminish her as a person in any way. If you find him with a new immediacy in the course of doing these exercises, anything may happen: anything, that is, except condemnation. He is, we need constantly to remind ourselves, the God of love.

People often ask for more explicit guidance in doing the exercises. It is impossible to give that guidance in general terms: so much depends on the individual's needs, aptitudes and preferences. Perhaps a few pointers may help, provided they are seen as no more than that: signposts, not a railway. First, the exercises – even a one-line suggestion that you recall a particular event in your life – nearly always take far longer than reading the chapter in which they are set. Of course some "come alive" for some people and others for others: but before concluding that this one isn't for you, may I ask that you give it plenty of time – and if necessary, come back to it two or three times? It may be permanently dead for you: or it may just be that it takes time to wake up. Even if an exercise seems full of possibilities for you, if it resonates well with your story, the temptation usually is to rush it . . . Let it take all the time it needs.

Second, it is often on the third or fourth repetition of an exercise that important new light is shed on the issue involved – and often quite unexpected light. It is as though something inside shifts, and you "see" from a new angle or gain a fresh perspective. Classical Islamic architecture depends upon you being in exactly the right spot. A yard to the left or right and you lose a whole series of arches leading through arches through arches . . . . That is not just a technical game: it is a profound statement in stone. Stand in the right place and look in the right direction, and you will have a splendid surprise: but you may have to pass this way often before you are thus rewarded.

Third, the exercises should take the form of a prayer: that is, they have the intention of bringing us more closely into a loving relationship with God. In the text that is not always made explicit. The "instructions" may only be to remember . . . or be aware of feelings . . . or imagine . . . . The danger is that that will be seen only as an invitation to intellectual or emotional activity. It is more than that: it is an invitation to *use* that material in a way that opens us to the love of God. One way of catching this is to start each exercise with a deliberate prayer. "Father, help me to draw closer to you as I reflect . . . or remember . . . or imagine . . . ." It is good, too, to get into the habit of finishing with a word of thanksgiving – even (perhaps particularly) if it has been a dry, unhelpful time. That, too, is a gift.

Fourth, if the exercises "do nothing" for you, do not imagine that you are a freak or a failure. Prayer is a funny business: it is unpredictable and inconstant. Not for nothing is the Spirit likened to the wind – here one moment, gone the next; blowing from the East now, from the South an hour ago, and from where by sundown? If this is not your way, that is my loss but a discovery for you. I hope the text will give you something while you continue your search for a style of prayer that is more naturally yours.

All these points imply that this is a book to be sucked slowly rather than gorged in one swallow. That is not because what I have to say is profound: I fear much of it is commonsensical to the point of banality. It is rather because the phrases on which the meditations are based reflect the peak of Paul's spiritual quest. It is to that that we must now turn.

(ii) The background

As I hinted earlier, what we know as the First and Second Letters to the Corinthians are almost certainly a number of letters or parts of letters put together and edited. This is not the place to go into the various theories about that editing process. It is enough for our purposes to accept that the first letter is probably more or less as Paul wrote it. The second letter, however, poses more of a problem. Although there is not scholarly unanimity on the issue, I tend to think that 2 Corinthians contains at least two, and possibly four, letters. Most importantly, chapters 10–13:10, remarkable for the severity, not to say bitterness, of their tone, were almost certainly written *before* chapters 1–9. What seems to have happened is this.

Paul visited Corinth for the first time on his second missionary journey, and subsequently wrote 1 Corinthians. As he forecast in that letter, he paid a second, quick visit to the city from Ephesus – a visit not mentioned in Acts. This visit seems to have been a disaster for Paul: he calls it "painful" (2 Corinthians 2:1). What precisely went wrong is not clear, but some of the difficulties can be deduced from the letter he wrote on his return to Ephesus, namely 2 Corinthians 10–13:10. Clearly an individual or clique, possibly someone very influential in civic affairs, had been bitterly critical of Paul. Ignoring both his accomplishments and his special status as an apostle – a status both awarded and validated by the events surrounding his conversion – his critics had accused him of arrogance, self-will, cowardice, avarice and hypocrisy. Further they had thought little of his preaching style, and urged the congregation at Corinth to have nothing to do with him. They may have had a favoured evangelist of their own and perhaps resented Paul's supplanting him.

Either way they seem to have called into question Paul's standing as an apostle, making out that he was in no way different from the many itinerant teachers and healers who passed through Corinth, poised as it was between east and west. To make matters worse, it seems as though many of the congregation at Corinth, many converted directly by Paul on his earlier visit, were disposed to support Paul's critics – or at the very least failed to stand by him when the criticism and associated gossiping started.

For Paul this represented not just a challenge to his authority, but a personal crisis. First, it called in question his whole missionary strategy. For all its evil reputation, Corinth's geographical position made it a key city in which to have an effective Christian presence, the more so since his visits to Athens and Thessalonica had been far from successful. He thought he had established such a presence. Now it was being subverted, not by external pressures but by those who claimed to "know Christ". The Church in Corinth was being destroyed by the very people who held the key to missionary expansion in Europe.

Second, these attacks caught Paul on the raw since they denied his vocation. They called into question his own understanding of himself in the light of his experience on the Damascus road, and they impugned his fitness as the leader of the mission to the Gentiles. That, in turn, played into the hands of his constant foes, the Judaizers – i.e. those who wanted to make Christianity a sect of Judaism.

Third, the critics ignored what had been achieved – and the cost it had exacted. Theirs was cheap criticism, destructive character assassination by those who had never taken the responsibility whose discharge they now condemned so loudly. Armchair critics can usually be ignored – but not when their criticisms are about to destroy not only a strategic element in a life-time's work but also the faithfulness of people who could not see through them.

Lastly, Paul was a human being. Tough as boots

physically, he was, like many such people, deeply sensitive, especially to criticism that, however unfair and exaggerated, had enough truth in it to make it sting. And it stung. One has only to read Chapters 10–13:10 in modern translation to feel the anger that only a strong man hit on a sore place can express.

Hurt, angry, desperately worried about the future of the whole European mission, and sickened by the small-mindedness of his critics, Paul sent his letter (2 Corinthians 10–13:10) via Titus, whom he hoped would reinforce his demand that his chief critic be punished. For that to be achieved, the majority of the Church would have to be shaken off the fence and mobilized to protect the purity of the Gospel Paul had preached.

It must have been a difficult time for Paul, waiting to hear whether he had won what had become a battle for survival at every level. Eventually he left Ephesus, probably having heard nothing, and set out for Corinth himself, hoping to meet Titus, who could bring him up to date with events in Corinth. Titus was not at the rendezvous, but met Paul later in Macedonia. To Paul's great relief, the news was good. The Church had swung behind him and the critics had been silenced. Paul immediately wrote 2 Corinthians 1–9: "From Paul, *Apostle* . . ." It is no surprise to find words like "consolation" and "comfort" falling over each other in repetition for the first seven verses. Out of the darkness of the previous months, light had at last appeared. He would bear the scar- tissue of the wounds inflicted by his critics for the rest of his life, but at least the Church and the wider mission were saved.

This long agony is central to an understanding of the verses we shall be considering in this book. For they are a historical representation, a time-warp, of the truth Paul wants to communicate: the power of God can do the impossible – bring joy out of sorrow, richness out of poverty, life out of death. Paul has experienced that as fact in the last months. He "knows" it, at the level of the inward knowledge of the heart, of the story of Jesus Christ, crucified and living. And he is living it every day as he continues his impossible task, buoyed by a Spirit who will not let him sink, even as the tide endlessly washes over him.

It is for that reason, I believe, that he presents us with a series of paradoxes. This is no literary device, used only to titillate the rhetorical appetites of his Hellenized audience, who would have been as familiar with the Stoic paradoxes as we are with the cliché lines of Shakespeare. It is lived truth. Paradox is the least inadequate vehicle for catching that quality of truth, because it can both hold in tension two opposites and simultaneously point to a resolution of those opposites that includes them but transcends them. More than that, it is, as it were, the natural language of discourse about a God who becomes man; a Saviour who is executed; a Redeemer who is tried in a frame-up by the civil and ecclesiastical powers; a Godhead that is one and three; a King whose Kingdom is here but to come, where royalty and humility are indistinguishable . . . . Only the language of paradox can cope with truth that constantly flirts with contradiction; with wisdom that easily implodes into foolishness. Only paradox can relate such fragile truth to the subtleties of experience reflected in faith.

May I then invite you to share your own paradox of the human condition, as we together explore Paul's experience of his?

2.

Impostors Who Speak The Truth

The first two paradoxes we shall be considering are different in form to the remaining four. In one sense they are not paradoxes so much as defensive denials in the spirit of his earlier letter (2 Corinthians 10–13:10) of charges that have been laid against Paul and his companions. We could read this first one then as: "You say we are impostors: in fact we are telling the truth." We do not know the substance of the charge. It may have been that some Christians at Corinth had heard of other evangelists, critical of Paul; maybe they had been in touch with the Church in Jerusalem, and had perhaps picked up some inkling of the tensions between Paul and it. In that case the charge of being an impostor would have been particularly hurtful, for it could suggest that it was not only in Corinth that his status as an apostle was being questioned.

Given the way he answers the charge – "We are telling you the truth" – it is more likely that the origin of this slur was less concerned with the acrimony between the various factions of the Church, which make its early history so accurate a harbinger of what was to follow, than with a more generalized dissatisfaction. Let us at any rate fantasize in that direction. Here was St Paul, we may suppose, preaching this strange new Gospel of love, peace, joy, harmony, reconciliation and, above all, humility. We may guess from his letters that in his daily preaching and teaching, he keeps returning to the astonishing, seemingly nonsensical fact that God assumed human form – already incredible – and died the death of an accursed criminal at the hands of the imperial power, a contradiction in terms so complete that many of his audience must have fallen about laughing at so ludicrous a religious confidence trick. He concludes from this fanciful notion that humility, giving way, giving up, letting pass, self-denial, readiness to yield to others — all these unJewish, non-imperial characteristics, are of the essence of God.

To the rough, tough, fast-living, hard-swearing folk of Corinth, this must have sounded not only improbable but also unattractive. Who wanted to be a universal doormat? Luckily it would be easy to discredit this part of Paul's message. "Look at him", we may hear them saying. "He talks about peace, patience and humility, but look at him. He's arrogant, divisive, harsh and brutal. Look at his second letter to us here in Corinth. Read between the lines, man. He talks of bringing a rod to us, this paragon of humility. He thinks he's beyond censure, this model of modesty. He is crudely critical of us, while puffing himself up with mock self-abasement. He calls us childish, and pretends to a fatherly authority over us. Not bad for someone who endlessly advocates taking the lower place. He criticizes us because there are cliques in the Church, but he brings nothing but dissension, with his rules for who prays and how they pray; for who eats what, for how we conduct the Lord's supper. . . ."

It is hard to read either his first or second letters to the Church in Corinth without being aware that Paul was not popular among substantial numbers, perhaps even a majority, there. Although he sometimes writes with tenderness and gentleness, often his tone is angry, bitter and hectoring. It is probable that his fury was directed at one particular group within the deeply divided Church, but, anxious to prevent the Church splitting into openly warring factions, he addresses the whole Church — hence harshness and love lie side by side.

This may well have added fuel to the fire of his critics. For it served to remind them both of the message of Paul, the quality of life he advocated, and of his reaction to the stories he had heard of life in the Church at Corinth since his visit there. His critics respond to his condemnation of their behaviour in a way that is instantly recognizable, indeed very modern. They call him a hypocrite. He stands for one thing and does another. He preaches one set of values and practises another. He can't live up to the standards he wants to inflict on others. He's no better than the quacks and trendies to be found at any frontier where two great cultures meet. Cut him down to size.

Paul was no doubt sufficiently stung by this charge, which reached him through that most faithful purveyor of hurtful gossip, the ecclesiastical grapevine, precisely because it had a grain of truth in it. He was capable of some unattractive outbursts, and if he could write like that — seemingly dictated to an amanuensis and therefore, we may assume, given due thought and consideration — one may be sure that in conversation, and particularly in dispute, he could be wounding and even offensive. It does not seem to me either honest or helpful to deny that; to gild the lily by emphasizing what is no doubt true — that only someone as tough as Paul could have survived the rigours of the missionary journeys that changed Christianity from a deviant sect of Judaism to a world religion. Let us face squarely the fact that Paul could be — and probably often was — arrogant, overbearing, dogmatic, impatient, intolerant and insensitive. So what?

It seems to me that when we face that honestly, two conclusions follow, both of which require of us further inner work.

The first is that, despite these warts, God was able to use Paul for one of the most significant ministries in the history of the Church. God does not demand of us that we become saints, least of all plaster saints or plastic saints, before he can use us. To put it another way, God knew that Paul had an unattractive side to his character before he revealed himself to him on the Damascus road. God could have chosen many other people, some of whom no doubt would have been more tolerant, patient and courteous with the dissidents and malcontents at Corinth and elsewhere. Nor do we need to adopt the pious conclusion that Paul *needed* these weaknesses of character, or that God made them into strengths. That does not seem to be true. He was rough when others might have been diplomatic. He was divisive when others might have been eirenic. He was prickly when others might have been suave. I prefer the ungilded, simple truth: Paul was a difficult, quick-tempered man, one who would in many offices and bureaucracies today be colloquially known as a bastard. Yet God not only accepted him, turned his life inside out (without making him much less of a bastard) and gave him all the gifts of the Spirit: he also entrusted to him one of the most dangerous but crucial tasks anyone has ever been given.

Let's look at that. Look first at your own weaknesses or deficiencies: that side of you that Jungians know as The Shadow. Unless you are unique – or uniquely lacking in self-awareness – you have become conscious over the years of bits of your make-up that you wish were otherwise. Would you care to recall those features now, not – emphatically not – in a spirit of self-judgement or condemnation. Ask to be shown them as they are, without exaggeration (which is an inverse form of pride) or dishonesty . . . Look at that shadow and thank God for it. You may not like it. He may not like it too much either. But it is part of you, and he made you as you are; and he loves and accepts and cherishes you as you are. The shadow is not to be shunned or feared or reviled or rejected. It has to be accepted, made friends with. One day no doubt it will change, perhaps even wither away. For the moment it is real – and really part of you. And it is no block to God's love for you . . . You might find it helpful to try to visualize your shadow as a person, namely you in all your negative guises. Then let that shadow meet Christ — in your sitting room or office or garden or over the washing up . . . How does Christ react? What does he say? . . . do? Stay with that as long as you can.

When we have come to terms with our own shadow and seen that it is accepted by Christ, we can come to terms with the shadow of other people. Very often our relationship with other people can be dominated by our consciousness of the shadow side of their personalities. We need to see that, however objectionable we may find their shadow, it is as readily accepted by Christ as is ours — and it is anyway the Shadow, not the substance. You may find it helpful to start with someone you know well, and do the same with their shadow as you did with your own: visualize it; and then sit it down with Christ . . . One word of warning. When we try to visualize the shadow of others, we are likely to be tempted in two directions. First, we may well project onto the other person some of our own shadow or our feelings about it, so that our imagined representation of the shadow of the other is actually a composite of what genuinely belongs to them and what really belongs to us. Second, we may find it harder to suspend criticism or condemnation when contemplating the shadow of others than when contemplating our own. "Yes, I know it's his shadow, but I really can't bear the way he . . ." It is usually enough to be aware of these difficulties to avoid them.

It is helpful to see the shadow of others through the eyes of Christ because it draws the sting out of the charge of hypocrisy. It enables us to accept that, yes, we are all hypocrites. No, none of us practises what he preaches. We may talk of the gifts of the Spirit, even in the language of the Spirit — and still see in ourselves and in others their very opposites: impatience for patience; sullenness for joy; intolerance for long-suffering, and so on. It is no surprise that St Paul says, no doubt in ironic tones, "We are the impostors who. . . ." Call us impostors, hypocrites if you like. And yes, you may well be right. We are both. How can we deny it? Why should we deny it? There is our shadow. We may regret him. We may want to see him disappear. But there he is — and he is as much accepted in Christ as any one else or as any other part of me.

When once we see that, we see too how hypocritical is the charge of hypocrisy! If we all have our shadows, what have we to criticize in others? "Ah, but *I* know I'm not perfect. So I don't keep going on about the faults and failings of others. . . ." And that takes us to Paul's rejoinder.

". . . . Impostors who speak the truth." The truth that Paul speaks is the shattering truth that the days of the shadow are numbered. "When anyone is united to Christ", he tells the Corinthians, "there is a new act of creation. His old life is over; a new life has already begun" (2 Corinthians 5:17, NEB variant reading). The new life offered "in Christ", through the power of God, is the life that will transform the shadow and make of the individual a new creature. This is the "message of reconciliation" that Paul offers the Corinthians, his friends and his critics alike. It is a message of reconciliation at two levels. As the "new creature" develops, so the old antagonism between self and shadow will disappear. The new life is a whole life, a life in which wholeness is experienced and real. And that wholeness, the work of God in Christ, makes it possible for us to become "one with the goodness of God himself". As long as we are dominated by or at war with our shadow that oneness with the goodness of God is impossible. God may *accept* our shadow as part of us, but it has gradually to be superseded by the new life that Christ makes possible. That new life will not instantly dispense with the shadow. Paul himself, as we have already seen, is proof enough of that. But it promises that the shadow will not rule our lives; that it will not finally separate us from that union with God for which we were created and for which God himself longs.

Hypocrite? Yes! Impostor? Yes! Paul can face the allegation with a confidence that comes from the truth he is anxious to share with anyone who will listen. What makes of any Christian a hypocrite and an impostor is not the final word. It is transitory, impermanent. For there is a power abroad that will eventually bring to fruit within us the wholeness and holiness of God himself. Bastards we may be. Gods we shall become.

We need to decide, don't we, whether we experience that as rhetoric or reality. John Fowles' book *The Magus* starts with the hero, Nicholas Urfe, summarizing his life so far: ". . . I was sent to public school, I wasted two years doing my national service, I went to Oxford; and there I began to discover I was not the person I wanted to be." That is a common enough experience — as is that of Urfe's twenty-three-year-old sleeping partner. She says to Urfe: "Don't you begin to feel things about yourself you know are you? Are going to be you for ever?" We are caught, aren't we, between Urfe's discontent with the person we are — and Alison's suspicion that we are that person for ever.

Paul's message surely is that Nicholas is right and Alison is wrong. We need not be caught. If we take our faith seriously, indeed we are not caught. For it is the core of that faith that the old life (Nicholas) is over — and, *pace* Alison, a new life has already begun.

Merely seeing this tension reflected in modern (and, at least at the superficial level, highly secular) literature does not tap into our own experience. Maybe, however, we can take Alison's question as the starting point of our own work. "Don't you . . . feel things about yourself you know are . . . going to be you for ever?" Or, to put it in a less despairing and more positive mode: "What things you know about yourself are you ready to have God change?" Back to the shadow, but this time, now that we know and accept it, we can see it less as a permanent feature of our existence, and more as the clay on which God can work. In doing so, he will not eliminate or destroy it — but rather subtly change its form and shape and texture, so that what was ugly becomes attractive; what was out of proportion becomes finely balanced; what was lop-sided or top-heavy becomes nicely turned. Will you, then, spend some time asking yourself my rephrasing of Alison's question: or, better, asking God to show you what you are ready to have changed? . . . This is not something to be rushed or "got on with". It is near the heart of the Christian life: let it take as long as it needs . . . Then tell God you are ready to have that changed; that that bit of shadow can go now. . . . and ask for trust that a new creature has been born. . . .

"We are the impostors who speak the truth." All Christians can say that — and say it, not with the defensive, ironic, controlled anger of Paul, but with the combination of humility and confidence that knows the worst but expects the best. Hypocrites we are: but we are on the way to liberation even from our own hypocrisy.

Summary of Exercises

1. Have a look at your Shadow. Thank God for it. Let it meet Christ.

2. Have a look at the Shadow of people close to you. Let it meet Christ.

3. What are you ready to have God change in you?

3.

Unknown Men Whom All Men Know

Of the six phrases this book is about, this one has caused me most trouble. On the face of it, it is a straight contradiction: "You call us unknown — in fact, everyone knows us." It could be that that is all there is to it. We need not expect every utterance of Paul to be pregnant with deeper meaning. As we have already seen, these phrases — this and the one before — are angrily denying a charge by his critics, and it could well be that that is all they are doing.

Before we abandon them as no more than a human reaction to criticism, however, two things need more careful consideration. First, it is highly improbable that Paul was particularly well known in Corinth or, with one or two exceptions like Ephesus, anywhere else. Why make a claim that is demonstrably false; and why make it immediately after having been accused of being an impostor, one, that is, who habitually makes claims that cannot be substantiated?

Second, the context hardly suggests a childish throw-away contradiction. Immediately Paul launches into an array of paradoxes that, so I shall argue, touch the deepest parts of both the human condition and the Christian faith. It is not impossible that he could slide from a "You are . . . I'm not . . . you are . . . I'm not" confrontation into a sequence of thought that encapsulates in a couple of dozen words the most profound elements of human experience. That itself would be a further paradox, not inconsistent with our line of thought in the previous chapter. Yet it remains so unlikely that I think we are obliged to look a little further. It is not much good turning to the commentaries and learned tomes. They are not, in this instance, much help, and anyway we need to relate what Paul has to say to our own experience. To do that, we need to fantasize a little, to use our imagination and the affective side of our minds at least as much as the analytical. I want to share with you my fantasy without in any way claiming that it is definitive or objectively "correct". What matters is what it touches in *you*, or rather enables to be touched in you.

It starts when as a small boy I was taken to London for the first time. I found it frightening, awe-inspiring, and utterly alien to anything I had ever known before. In this frame of mind I was taken, one winter evening, to Westminster Abbey. The last of the daylight was fading and, perhaps for reasons of economy — for this was not long after the end of the Second World War, when austerity was a natural way of life as well as a legal requirement — the Abbey was so dimly lit that the light itself seemed grey, almost apprehensible.

Near the West Door, however, was a group of very grand soldiers. To me they looked both magnificent and forlorn, like great galleons dried out in a muddy harbour. They wore full-dress uniform, with swords by their sides, medals on their chests reflecting what little light there was. With both fascination and horror, I saw that some had spurs on their heels. Yet there was nothing of the pomp and bombast and braggadocio of the military men I'd seen strutting through our Yorkshire village on VE day. They stood in a small raggedy knot, heads bowed, silent. There was something in the air that precisely matched the gloom of this dark, empty, nearly silent building on a November evening. You could almost touch it, smooth but hard, warm, damp — my mother's fur coat after she had been caught in a storm.

A light began to burn in the middle of the group of soldiers. It was not the hard, pricking light of the pairs of bare bulbs high in the roof of the Abbey. No, it was a glowing, pinkish light that reminded me of the night-lights my mother put by my bedroom door when I was sick. The military men seemed even more intent, even more silent, their ranks drawn even tighter. My father froze. I pressed against him. . . . Then they were gone. With barely a sound, they seemed to float away through the West Door and into the night. Only the glowing pink lamp remained.

"What is it?" I breathed to my father, alarmed at how loud I sounded.

"The tomb of the Unknown Soldier", he whispered and I could see in his face and hear in his voice the same fur-coat feel that was sadder than the saddest thing I had ever known.

"What's that? . . . Who is he?" He was obviously terribly important to have all those medals and swords and spurs round him. And in silence.

My father looked away and then turned round to face me. He had his back to the light and I could only see his silhouette. But his voice was different.

"He's . . . he's all of us.'

The unknown man who is all of us. The anonymous victim who represents each of us. It is a deeply Old Testament idea, from the scapegoat which carries the sins of the community into the desert, to the priest who, unnamed and unimportant himself, represents the people in the Holy of Holies, and risks encounter with the living God in the process. In what sense, if any, does Paul stand in this tradition? Or, to put it another way, in what respects can we see Paul as representative of all of us? How is he "known by all men" in the sense of allowing everyone to say "He is all of us"?

This question invites us deep into Paul's spiritual journey. We are not concerned here with Paul the missionary or Paul the ecclesiastical administrator or Paul the relief fund raiser. Those are external activities by which a deeper personality is expressed. It is the process of the transformation of that personality that we need to recapture.

The contrast between the persecuting Saul and the caring, sustaining, evangelizing Paul is so well known that it is in danger of becoming a cliché. Nor is it, as a matter of fact, all that unusual; history is studded with poachers turned gamekeepers, and vice versa. Much less usual and much more central to our purpose is Paul's consciousness of being engaged on a spiritual journey – but a journey that is maddeningly slow and frustrating.

For as much of the year as I can manage, I live in a remote valley in mid-Wales. The nearest shop is four miles away, and the nearest telephone a brisk twenty-minute walk. It is not, as you may say, on the beaten track. That has great advantages: but it makes travelling to and fro, in the absence of a car, an exercise in neglect of the clock. The journey starts with a lift to our nearest market town from my neighbouring farmer. He works on what is known locally as "PGT". It took me a few months to summon up courage to enquire what PGT is. "Well, boy, it's the opposite of Greenwich *Mean* Time, see? Powys Generous Time." Luckily the bus company operates on PGT, too. So the ten o'clock bus to Hereford is likely still to be waiting when my neighbour drops me at the bridge at 10.20 or 10.50. When it does leave, the bus wanders beautifully but circumambulatorily eastwards, making whatever detours the driver's intuition, and helpful suggestions from his passengers, may prompt. It usually works. By the time we are finally over the border, the bus is full and progress can accelerate . . . until the next leg, when the meanderings of the bus company are replaced by the vagaries of British Rail – British Rail, that is, operating a branch line it would much rather close. The question is not whether the train will be on time: the question that exercises the handful of nervous passengers is whether it will run at all; and in what direction, if any. By the time I reach London, I decide that maybe GMT has something to be said for it.

Now when I make that journey I see it as an allegory both of St Paul's life and of the Christian life in general.

Here was a man, after all, who had had a shattering conversion experience. We do not need to prod that experience too closely: what is clear is that he went through a spiritual and psychological trauma that left him a changed man. He would never forget his past: it would haunt and humble him for the rest of his life, but having been baptized and having received the Holy Spirit, he was conscious of his personality changing so fast and so radically that he constantly talked of baptism being (not representing or symbolizing, but actually constituting) a new quality of life. The essence of that quality of life, Paul discovered, was love, the very reverse of the persecuting hatred he had hitherto shown the Christian heretics, among whom he was now proud to be numbered. As a good Jew he was not unfamiliar with the notion of love as a key ethical and religious principle: much of the law is, after all, about love in action. Now, however, he was enabled to live it, imperfectly, haltingly, inadequately. Yet he could live it deeply enough and costingly enough to be able to write a hymn on love that is one of the greatest spiritual songs of any age in any language.

It is as haunting as it is, however, because it is a hymn of longing rather than a celebration of accomplishment. It is because Paul knows that he is not yet perfectly patient; not yet never boastful; not yet sure of keeping no score of wrongs; not yet, in a word, as loving as the King of Love; it is because he is not yet all these things that he can hold the ideal to which he aspires so tantalizingly before us. And he knows it. "My knowledge now is partial; then it will be whole, like God's knowledge of me."

I suggest that it is this partiality; this on-the-way-but-not-yet-there quality of Paul's life and lived experience that makes him "known to everyone". Before we go on to look at its most complete statement, would you care to spend a little time reflecting on your own experience of this sense of incompletion? In a way this is a continuation of the work we were engaged in in the last chapter. There we were reflecting on what parts of our shadow we were now ready to let go. Now it might be good to reflect on that as *process*. If I look at strata of my life, how I was ten years ago, five years ago, two years ago, can I detect parts of me that have perhaps begun to change? One way of getting a lock on this is to recall an incident from the middle-distant past that made you unhappy with yourself: an occasion perhaps in which you felt you had somehow not been true to your deepest self, to the real you. Now ask yourself how would you handle it today if the same situation arose. It is easy of course to say: "Ah, I've learnt by my mistakes." It is not what we have learnt that really matters, however. It is what we are. So try to see what you are now — in that hypothetical situation — and compare it with what you were in that actual situation.

Clearly the object of this exercise is not to lead us to say: "Wow! I *have* come a long way." That may well be true: indeed it certainly will be true if we have been allowing the Spirit even a toehold in our lives. No, the object is to look forward as well as back, to see that we are caught up in a process that still has a way to go. So now repeat the exercise — and ask yourself what Christ would have done in the situation now. How do you think he would have reacted? What would he have said? have done? . . . As you reflect on that, you might like to re-read Paul's hymn of love (1 Corinthians 13), substituting "Christ" for the word "love" . . . We are likely to find, aren't we, that while we may, thank God, have come some way in the journey to which we are called, we have still a long road ahead before we shall routinely practise perfect love.

I suspect few of us need convincing of that! More frequent is the reaction of a young friend the other day: "Charles, I get so *bored* of my failings. I sometimes long to go off for a dirty weekend or rob a bank or tell my boss exactly what I think of her. . . . It wouldn't do much for the Kingdom, but it would certainly make a pleasant change from these. . . ." and she made a despairing gesture, as though at a line of washing. Paul would have known exactly what she meant. You can hear the throb of frustration in his voice: "The good that I would I do not. And the evil I would not, that I do. . . . Who can deliver me from this body of death . . .?" (Romans 7:19,24).

Isn't that where we so often find ourselves? "What," said somebody else, "whatever is the *matter* with me? As I do it, I know I shouldn't . . . that I will regret it. Yet I don't seem able to resist it. Is there something wrong with me?" The answer, I suppose, is yes and no. There is something radically wrong: but it is true of us all.

You might like to reflect on when you last found yourself saying or thinking something along these lines: "The good that I would, I do not. The evil that I would not. . . ." It is, if you like, the power of Shadow. It is real. And it is enduring. It is well to be aware of it. But, as we saw in the last chapter, it is not unchangeable. And we have already seen that change is happening. Can you hold those two in tension: the power of Shadow; and the greater power of Christ to change Shadow? A meditative image I find helpful – and if you have or can develop one of your own that means more to you, use it – is that of a stream. However long the water may be held in a pool, the stream cannot deny the pull of gravity. That pull is always present – invisible, inapprehensible, but undeniable. The water *will* reach the sea; even though the pool is still and deep and dark. . . .

Perhaps it seems we have come a long way from St Paul. Perhaps we have. Yet I do not think so – unless there was a major break in his thought. We have progressed from "speaking the truth" to being "known by all men"! If I am right, that Paul was "known" by all men as one who represents for us the pain and hopefulness of spiritual adolescence, of the partiality of our present knowledge, then it is no surprise to find his next thought going yet deeper into Christian paradox. Caught between the powers of death and the promise of life, indeed experiencing the reality of that promise in baptism and the gift of the Spirit, he can find the confidence to look death in the eye. "Dying – and we live on." It is that central paradox that will occupy us for some time now.

Summary of Exercises

1. What changes do you see in your life and personality over the last ten years? five years? two years?

2. What processes do you think were at work in those changes?

3. If you can recall a particular instance in the past when you now think you were not faithful to your truest self, "replay" that event with Christ taking your role.

4. Read 1 Corinthians 13, substituting "Christ" for "love".

5. Hold in meditative tension the power of the Shadow ("the good that I would I do not . . .") and the power of Christ to change the Shadow.

4.

Dying — And We Live On

We have already seen that Paul wrote this letter in a state of near euphoria. He had met Titus on the road in Macedonia. Titus had told him that his second letter had been well received; that his accusers had been silenced; that he himself would be well received if he now continued on his journey to Corinth. . . . A huge load of anxiety and self-doubt was lifted from his shoulders. He could come alive again to all the creative possibilities that a Christian community at Corinth offered; he could be alive again to the warmth and affection of people he had baptized in the power of the Spirit. Life, it must have seemed, had come at last from a deathly situation.

That may well be some of the background to this central paradox. It is not, however, the essence of what St Paul is saying. He is not affirming that life can sometimes follow what looks like death; that light follows shade. Many Greek philosophers would have agreed with that. He is saying something much more profound — and much more paradoxical: namely that life is found *in* death: that it is the process of death that gives birth to life; or that death cannot finally extinguish the possibility of life.

That is so startling and improbable a claim that it surely deserves exploring. Can it *really* be true that death brings life; that defeat and failure can open new opportunities for growth and development? Such a notion would strike most of our contemporaries as hogwash. A Marxist or hedonist or humanist would scoff at the idea that personal suffering and death can bring new shoots of creative growth. We are not, then, dealing with ideas that are part of our contemporary culture. We are back to the biblical roots of the Christian faith. Where, then, is the evidence?

1. Let's start with what T. S. Eliot calls "lesser deaths". I guess we have all at some stage experienced rejection, acute disappointment, a terrible sense of loss of a valued part of ourselves, our family or our environment – a sense of loss that is much like a bereavement.

The whole story of the Old Testament is founded on such an experience. Have that is to say, the experience of a sudden parting from all that was secure and comfortable and worthwhile and good. Before we look at that, you may find it helpful to reflect for a few moments on your own experience. Have there been moments, periods, in your life which seemed like a lesser death: when you found yourself being parted from all kinds of things that you formerly set great store by? Recall that period now. Don't try to intellectualize it, analyse it. Rather just *feel* it: recall how you felt as one thing after another was taken from you. . . . Remember the anger, the resentment, the self-pity. . . . Or the lostness, the puzzlement: why me? . . . How did it feel?

You were never alone in that reaction. It is as old as religious consciousness.

"Yahweh said to Abram: 'Leave your country, your family and your father's house for the land I will show you'" (Genesis 12:1).

We are in the land where myth and history meet – something like the Norse sagas, or the Mabinogion of Wales. Was there a historical figure actually called Abram? Did he set out from Ur or Haran? What made him do so?

We can answer none of those questions with any degree of confidence. Perhaps that does not matter too much. For what is clear is that we have here a folk memory of religious awareness. The author of this portion of Genesis is giving an account of the religion of his people; of what he thought would convey in story the realities of the faith of the people. And what were those realities?

That God offers horrendous challenges: "Leave . . . and I will." He is not a Moloch God making insatiable demands for sacrifices that he will consume, and then come back for more. So he is remembered not just as a God who says "Leave": but as a God who says, "Leave – for the land I will show you."

It is the leaving that is the hard bit, isn't it? Put yourself now in Abram's shoes. There he is, well established in Haran. To transpose it into our terms, he's got a comfortable home, a nice little semi- on a '60s estate, a good job with the local authority and a brand new Maestro. He's married to this attractive, vivacious girl Sarah, whom everyone likes and admires. They don't actually have any children, and their closest friends know that this is a bit of a disappointment, but they certainly haven't given up trying. A bit of peace and quiet, time for Sarah to relax and stop worrying about things, and maybe the one gap in their lives will be filled. Even without that, they're a happy, well-adjusted couple, universally popular, forever being invited out, already taking a lead in the community. Their future is certainly bright, with Abram's promotion in the pipe-line, the mortgage reducing month by month, and Sarah starting to help in the local nursery school.

Then crunch. Yahweh says: "Leave. . . ."

"Leave? Do I have to leave? Me? Why me? Why should I . . .?"

"Leave!"

"But what about Sarah? You know she needs a quiet, settled time if she's going to have a better chance of. . . ."

"Leave!"

"It's all right saying leave – but where do we go?"

"Leave – and I will show you . . ."

Try completing the conversation. *Be* Abram, suddenly

faced with this challenge. What do you say to Yahweh? And what do you think he would say to you? Can you try that?

*

I wonder what came up then? There's no "right" answer, of course. I can only tell you what came up for me — resentment, anger, a sense of injustice. Resentment because I am comfortably settled and the last thing I want now is to be unsettled. Anger because my own private world, which I've preserved so carefully, is going to be blown to bits. And a sense of injustice because I don't see why it should all happen to *me*. Why me? There's John Smith down the road, Lord, why not him?

There is something else too; this half-promise: ". . . the land I will show you." I am not sure how to interpret that. Certainly, I'm extremely reluctant to pack up, put the house on the market, sell my new car, leave a secure job with an inflation-proofed pension, on the back of a promise like that. I might try to persuade the Lord to arrange an inspection flight, like the smart West-End estate agents who sell houses in Spain or the Caribbean.

If I'm honest, I'm reluctant for another reason. I might not like this new land. What guarantee is there that it is better than what I've got? Sarah and I are very happy here. We've worked hard to make the home nice, licked the garden into shape, made friends with the neighbours, found a niche in the parish church. It may not be perfect but it's all we've ever wanted, and we really don't want to be sent off on some wild goose chase to a land we might not like so well.

So here I am, faced not with one lesser death, but a whole Death Row of them. I've got to die to that security I value so highly. I've got to give up all I've worked for, all I've built up around me, all I've invested my whole personality in. Then I've got to give up control. If I do leave, I'm no longer in control of my own life – and I find that hard, perhaps hardest of all because it is a death to self at the deepest level. It implies that I have got to die even to my own hopes. I'm looking forward to that promotion, to at last having status and prestige. Most of all Sarah and I are looking forward to kids. Leaving is a death to that, too. So it's not just a death to my self: it's a death to our children yet unborn.

Here we have a recognition, in the early religious consciousness of the people of God, that Yahweh's call – "Leave" – can be a death. Yet the same religious consciousness invites us to believe that we may stand that on its head: a death, a lesser death, can be the call of God. I say "can be", not "always is". Some lesser deaths seem devoid of meaning, devoid of the possibilities of growth.

That is one of those miserable facts of the human situation. It is balanced, however, by the fact that *some* pain, suffering, deprivation *is* indeed a situation out of which Yahweh calls us forward – and my hunch is that God calls, or tries to use, many more of our lesser deaths in this redemptive way than we will give him credit for.

Perhaps you know the symptoms from your own experience. We suffer a disappointment, a loss, a rejection, a blow, and we sit in a heap of self-pity bemoaning the fact that this cruel God of ours could have dealt us such a blow. Slowly, maddeningly slowly, we begin to realize that out of the disappointment, the pain, something new is beginning to emerge. We have lost a prized possession or status or position . . . but now the perspectives are changing. Not only does it no longer look all that important; we are being drawn to something else of far greater value.

That is not, of course, an essentially Christian or religious insight. George Eliot explores it in entirely secular terms in *Silas Marner*. Silas starts as a hard-working weaver who has allowed his ample savings – about

£50,000 in today's terms — to dominate his whole life and personality. He is, in a word, a miser. The money is stolen and Silas is broken. He cannot cope with being suddenly reduced to poverty. At this moment of abandonment, he takes in a baby girl and grows into a warm, gentle, unselfish foster father. Death to money is followed by life to a human relationship of a quality Silas the miser had never conceived.

The Old Testament belief is that this transition is neither unusual nor random. It is not unusual, in the sense that it is of the nature of Yahweh to deprive in order to enrich. And it is not random, in the sense that the purposes of God may indeed be glimpsed in and through this process.

Thus the editor of this part of the Genesis tradition is clear that Yahweh's promise to Abram points towards a profound spiritual truth. He does that by a simple literary device. He portrays Yahweh saying to Abram: Leave all this you have accumulated in Haran and I will make you so happy that people will say to each other: "May you know happiness like that of Abram."

It is no surprise to discover then that this juxtaposition of "leave" and "I will" recurs throughout the biblical record, in the New Testament as well as the Old. It is a repeated theme in Jesus' own ministry: Follow me and I will make you . . . Give away all you have and come. . . . Leave self behind and come. . . . Inevitably it is a theme, perhaps the theme, that he lives out most explicitly. He leaves the relative safety of Galilee; leaves all security; dies; and is made alive. The deepest conviction of Genesis is given final validation.

As we have already seen, from many different angles, Paul's life also attests it. He dies to all his authority, respectability, self-esteem and spiritual security as a Pharisee: and it is a traumatic and painful business doing so. Yet he finds he is given something so precious that all he has given up seems rubbish by comparison.

In our over intellectualized, highly rationalized culture, it is hard for us to repossess this core truth of the Judaeo-Christian experience of God. Leave ... and I will. ... We find it almost impossible to trust that. We want to probe it with our intellects; to calculate the risks; to look for guarantees. We have to learn, I believe, to switch out of the mode of the intellectual – the mind – into the mode of the affective, emotional, imaginative – the heart – if we are to nourish what slender resources of trust we can muster. The mind will never apprehend the truth of paradox. Only the heart can do that. And here we are at the centre of paradox.

2. That paradox has many layers. One of the most puzzling in the Christian life is what has come to be called the desert experience – the discovery, that is, that just as we are beginning to respond, however uncertainly and timidly to that first invitation "Leave ...", we find that so far from being led immediately into a land flowing with milk and honey, we are dumped in the middle of a desert.

Looking back on their history from the relatively fertile lands of the Jordan Valley and the coastal plains, the people of Israel remembered with horror their home in the desert. I have been in a physical desert only twice – once in West Africa and once in Southern Namibia. It is a deeply disturbing environment – the emptiness, the flatness, the sameness, mile after mile of it. The occasional bit of dried up scrub; or thin, wiry grass, burnt grey by the sun; a rare fold in the sand or a glimpse of a distant ridge – that's it. Silence. Emptiness. Aridity. You can easily imagine it would drive you mad even before it dried you out ... I remember returning from South Namibia to our little house in a remote Welsh valley. My neighbour, a sheep farmer, was in despair after six rainless weeks. "Terrible, isn't it?" he complained. "It's as dry as a stove." All I could see were green trees, fields of lush grass, streams, fat sheep and the most beautiful landscape in the world.

The Israelites must have felt something like that – even in the hot Mediterranean summer. They had a folk memory of what the desert was like, just how terrible it could be; how utterly *other* to their present comfortable existence in the green valleys of Jordan.

To relate their memory to yours, would you like to recall desert experiences you have had, times when you seemed to be stuck in an inner landscape of emptiness, dryness; times when you looked back and longed to be where you felt safe and secure, even though you may have been trapped, a spiritual and emotional slave? You may have gone through such a time after a particular trauma, when the wounds simply refused to heal. Or it might have come out of a clear blue sky, unassociated with any particular event. Can you recall the inner pain, when you seemed deserted, left to fend for yourself in the desert? Try to recapture that now.

*

Did you find that very painful? If so, it might be some comfort to discover that that is the experience of the ages – from the communities of scholar-saints out of which the Old Testament emerged, to modern masters of the spiritual life. A contemporary Australian master had this to say as he reflected on his own experience of watching his twenty-year-old daughter die of leukaemia – and then being driven out into the desert by grief, bitterness, anguish and anger. "I doubt whether any person who genuinely follows Christ as the pathfinder avoids the desert experience: it is one of the trademarks of the spiritual life. We might want God to say to us, 'All is well and you won't get hurt', but while that may be true in an ultimate sense, it is transparently true in this temporal order of things that all is not well, and that we are certain to get hurt. Jesus was hurt. What right have you and I to ask for immunity? To do so is to ask for cheap grace, to avoid the costs of discipleship" — words borrowed from someone who perhaps knew the desert better than most, Dietrich Bonhoeffer.

How do people cope in that inward desert — in those moments, months of lostness and dereliction? Again, I think the authors of Exodus, reflecting on the folk memory of a real experience, give us some pointers. The first is about only moving when you're sure you have to. The temptation is to try to compensate for that sense of lostness, of confusion, of inner loneliness by roving around, being hyperactive, trying to *do* something. We even cease to care much precisely what we do, so long as we achieve *something*. Such is the nature of manic compensation. Indeed, I sometimes wonder if there is a correlation between the depths of spiritual life and the temptation to react to the desert by such compensation. It is as though a spiritual energy is being frustrated, dammed up. It needs to explore every possibility, every fissure, constantly searching for a way through. Deeper wisdom suggests patience.

In a letter to a favourite niece Baron von Hügel had three analogies which have always helped me — not least, I suppose, because they are drawn from activities I enjoy. Thus von Hügel takes the example of a sailor caught in a storm. As any good manual on seamanship will tell you, the most sensible thing to do, if you have enough sea-room, is not to try to fight the storm, but to ride it out, expending as little energy as possible. Take down the sails. Put out a sea anchor. Batten down the hatches. And go below to rest. Sleep if you can. Be sure the storm will blow itself out. You will need all your resources to continue your voyage thereafter.

Or if you are on a mountain and the cloud comes down, rolling in those grey billows that can in minutes transform a warm afternoon and a spectacular view into a chilling, damp world of a few square yards and great uncertainty: what then? Surely you do not set off at a brisk pace in the direction you *think* leads down the mountain. That can be, quite literally, suicidal. You make what shelter you can, and keep as warm and as dry as you can. Von Hügel would have approved of the recommendations of a recent study of survival techniques in such a situation. One advises a "positive mental attitude" (don't whinge or panic or despair). Another suggests "shared bodily warmth" (snuggle up close to your fellow mountaineers, because you are more likely to survive together than you are to survive alone).

Von Hügel's third analogy, of which I can claim no direct experience, is a sandstorm in a literal desert. A nomad does not try to continue his journey. Rather he lies face down, feet to the wind, and, drawing a blanket over him, he waits for the storm to blow itself out, aware that by the time it does so he may be covered in several inches of sand.

These three parables have this in common: they are about waiting for the environment to change – but waiting positively, with the expectation that change it will: knowing that the journey will be resumed (albeit possibly from a different position); and knowing that the journey ahead will require resources that should not be frittered away by useless or even dangerous activity now.

We see this same acknowledgement of the dangers of spiritual panic and ill-judged decisions associated with it, in the biblical record of the desert experience of Israel. You remember how they were led by the cloud during the day and the pillar of fire by night? In the last chapter of the book, the authors of Exodus remind us that the Israelites followed the cloud only when it moved: "The Israelites moved their camp to another place only when the cloud lifted from the Tent. As long as the cloud stayed there, they did *not* move their camp."

The spiritual experience of the authors and their community, then, was that in the desert you stay put unless you are firmly, even visibly moved on. Scuttering about – whether physically or spiritually – like so many terrified rats in a burning house will only lead to disaster. To change the image, in his study of the Psalms – revealingly entitled *A Cry of Absence: Reflections for the Winter of the Heart* – Martin Marty sees the desert not in terms of heat and glare, but in terms of the total freeze-up of the northern states of America. He sees the Psalmist (in Psalm 88) caught in that great winter freeze: "O Lord my God, by day I call for help, by night I cry aloud in thy presence . . . for I have had my fill of woes and they have brought me to the threshold of hell." "Such times", says Marty, "suggest a frozen Niagara Falls, a stalactitic maze of frozen drops forming a curtain to defeat the seeker on a spiritual journey."

You stay put – because you need to; or because you can do nothing else. It's not all passive, however. Again the authors of Exodus, looking back on the inner reality of the desert experience, knew how powerful are the temptations to compromise, to give up, to ease the pain of the desert by over-indulgence or self-satisfaction. They represent that reality by the symbol of the Baalim, the false gods (and goddesses) of the heathen tribes with whom the Israelites came into contact. Here were gods and goddesses who were worth having. They guaranteed you a good time: they encouraged you to drink too much; to fornicate freely; to settle down into a comfortable rut; to eat, drink and be merry. Why put on the hair shirt? they mocked. Why not enjoy the fullness of the land? So Moses warns the people that flirting with the Baals could "be a fatal trap for you . . . when they worship their pagan gods and sacrifice to them, they will invite you to join them and you will be tempted to eat the food they offer to their gods." It is always a temptation to run out of the desert at the wrong level, as it were; to kill its pain, to substitute the real winter by a spring we make for ourselves.

That is usually the response of despair. Feeling abandoned, we abandon. We abandon our commitment to the journey. We abandon hope that it will be resumed. We abandon the possibility that it will one day be completed. So why not make the best of a bad job and throw in our lot with the Baalim of our day?

It is often helpful to be able to put a finger on our own Baalim, for once known for what they are, their capacity to hurt us is much reduced. So you might like to spend a little time trying to identify those Baalim in your own life. When you are near to despair about the spiritual journey on which you are engaged; in those times of dryness, depression and deadness, what is it that looks exciting, life-giving — but which the deepest part of you knows is somehow false? You may be able to recall directly some such experience. Or you may prefer to come at it through the use of your imagination.

Suppose you are abroad in a far distant country, unknown to you. You are quite alone; the people you were coming to meet failed to get your message and are many miles up-country, quite out of contact. The city is suddenly gripped by a general strike, so your movements are severely limited. All flights are fully booked for the next two weeks and no one can guarantee you a seat even then. (If, incidentally, this scenario seems far-fetched, it is almost exactly the situation in which I currently find myself as I write these lines.) You are, however, staying in a comfortable hotel that has every facility imaginable, from libraries to discotheques; from bars to swimming pools; from cinemas to sports complexes. You can, in a word, do what you like — except go home, meet your friends or move around. First of all, decide how you would cope with the situation. How would you spend your time, not in the first day or two while you are exploring the possibilities — but by the end of the second week? . . . Please do not judge yourself harshly: that is not the point. Merely try to see how you would cope with the loneliness and the frustration. . . . Then suppose that you meet Jesus in the lobby of the hotel after two weeks. What does he say to you: and what do you say to him?

That exercise may or may not help you identify the particular Baalim that might afflict you in the desert. The final part of the exercise, however, is the key. For however much we resent the desert, however much we rail against its hellish quality, the settled conviction of the authors of Exodus, and of all mystical writers since, is that God is there in the desert with us. It is not that he pushes us out to endure the emptiness, the loneliness, the meaninglessness while he gets on with something more important; much less that he gets some kind of satisfaction from watching us writhe in pain or simply die on our feet – or on our knees. No, the conviction of the authors of the Exodus is that he is there, with them, sharing their wanderings, their experience of strangeness, and their alienation.

This conviction is given striking expression in the folk memory of Exodus. So sure is that memory of Yahweh's presence that it recalls Yahweh's astonishing words: "The people must make my home among them." Here is the central symbol of God's at-one-ness, at-home-ness, with his people even as they wander, frightened, uncertain and lost, half-longing for the old certainties of slavery. They call that symbol "The tent of his presence" and it comes to represent his loving care for them in all their vicissitudes. It is hard for us to recapture the scale of religious inventiveness or, if you like, the majesty of revelation that this conviction betokens. The terrible, unapproachable God, whose presence is so awesome that it consumes good and bad alike – such a God is not denied, but that image is balanced by a God who travels with his nomadic people, who shares their simple life, who can, as it were, contain his majesty in the small space of a desert traveller's tent, in order that he may always be where his people are.

Lucky for them, we may say. There's no Tent of His Presence in Cheam or Chudleigh, or Wigan, or Workington. There's just me and my pain; me and my inner emptiness. I know. And that is the horrendous paradox at the heart of the Christian faith. As Thomas Merton, perhaps one of the great saints of this century, put it: "The person searching for the depths seems universally to be led into a place where there seems nothing tangible to rely upon, no conflicts, no rewards, sometimes no peace – in fact one could sometimes believe, no God."

It's tough in the desert. It's bewildering. It's destructive. It's hellish. Yet the testimony of the Old Testament, and ever more strongly, of the New, is that out of it comes new growth, new insight, new certainty that a God of love is at home among us. Martin Marty concludes his study of the winter of the heart like this: "A wintry sort of spirituality produces occasions when the Absence leaves the horizon and Presence realizes itself. 'The Lord is close to those whose courage is broken and he saves those whose spirit is crushed' (Psalm 34:18). The Presence then comes so close that you can sense it. On the wintry landscape, the searcher hears psalms sung, sees pilgrim bands, smells the incense of restored prayer, touches the company of the faithful – and even tastes. . . . The Psalmist had a word for that, too, a promise after the fallow season. 'Taste, then, and see that the Lord is good' (Psalm 34:8). One hopes." One certainly does. The winter of the heart is followed by the spring of Easter. One hopes.

3. It would, I suspect, be a valid objection to the story so far that it interpreted the basic theme of life being brought out of death purely in an individual sense. That objection would be made the more telling by the fact that the Old Testament often puts this faith into a corporate or group

setting. It is not only the life of an individual rediscovered in the death of that individual: it is the life of a community rediscovered in the death of that community. The desert experience of the people of Israel, for example, was just that: an experience of the whole people, and it was the whole people who discovered a faith that God had come to make his home with them — even in the desert.

So the biblical record invites us to expect for communities what it also teaches us to expect for individuals. Can we make any sense of that? Is it really possible? Or is it just a pious platitude?

First, let's try to be clear about what sort of communities we have in mind. The Old Testament is the story of the people of God, that is to say, the particular ethnic group who became convinced that God had made a Covenant or Pact with them. They sometimes called themselves the covenanted people, the people with whom God had chosen to have a particularly close bond.

So we have to look for the community of which that is true today, and the extraordinary thing is that, so we Christians believe, God has actually chosen as his new people this funny — sometimes not so funny, sometimes tragic — persistently failing, institution, the Church. However bizarre it may seem — and to me at least it often seems very bizarre indeed — God chose the Church, the community of people who confess Christ as Lord, as his people with whom he entered into a specially close relationship. And if that kind of language reminds you of a torrid romance as reported in the downmarket dailies, that should come as no great surprise. From the earliest times a metaphor for the Church has been the bride of Christ — a special relationship indeed.

The question we have to ask, then, is whether or in what sense life is brought out of death in the Church? We need to start, I think, with the Church we know, as it really is to us. I wonder how *you* experience the Church? — as an institution that is dead and deathly — or as one that is alive and life-giving? As the bride of Christ — or as a sour old maid? A community that *could* come alive — or as one in which rigor mortis is well advanced? Don't analyse it, debate it. Just become aware of your feelings over it — and don't be frightened of being honest about it.

I wonder what you found when you allowed those feelings in? I'm constantly surprised and dismayed at how many people have been *hurt* by the Church — and I don't mean only obvious groups like women, who are denied the opportunity to test their vocation to the priesthood, or divorcees, who at the precise moment of their lives when they most need the assurance of forgiveness, acceptance and encouragement, find themselves being given the frozen shoulder. I mean people of all sorts who look to the Church for a glimpse of the loving generosity of God, and instead find an institution that is, as they experience it, neither loving nor generous. We Christians have little to be proud of, it seems to me, in the way we live our conviction that God has chosen the Church as his bride, his partner, his lover.

And yet miracles do happen — and I don't say that lightly. It takes a miracle, doesn't it, to transform a deathly institution into a life-support system — or a Church that diminishes women and men into one that enables them to encounter their Lord at the deepest part of themselves.

The story I want to tell is like that — but different. It isn't in fact about a church that was dead in the conventional sense, for in that respect this particular church was successful. Indeed that was exactly its problem. It was a show-place — membership high and rising; giving going up; activities galore. When a new minister was appointed, he was told he was taking over one of the best churches on the eastern seaboard of the USA.

There was, however, one fly in the ointment. Right across the river from the church was a shipyard where nuclear submarines were built. Indeed, many of the congregation were employed in the yard or in the naval training facility associated with it. Hitherto that had been a taboo subject. Church life and everyday life were kept at arm's length from each other, and so both could prosper – sort of. The new minister found a few people in the church who were not too comfortable at this stand-off; who thought that maybe Christian discipleship did in fact involve finding the right connection between the two. So a study group was set up to look at a responsible Christian attitude to the armaments industry. Some people were hurt, others outraged, that such a question should be asked. They were hurt and outraged when the study group reported to the church meeting that it was incompatible with Christian obedience to be involved in any way with the production or delivery of nuclear weapons.

Uproar! The church divided. Many people left. A few, however, got a whiff of something that was new and exciting – the idea that the Christian faith is not a set of abstract propositions demanding assent, nor participation in a series of religious concerts, but rather an encounter with a lovable, attractive Person who knows you inside out if you give him half a chance – and in the process shows you a whole new perspective on the world and on yourself.

This small minority were put under enormous pressure by those who wanted to preserve the status quo, who wanted a successful church. Despite such pressure, which included abusive telephone calls, ostracism, and persecution at work, they began to see the scale of the new obedience into which they were being led. They resigned from the shipyard and the navy. They began to share their savings and their homes, initially with each other and then with the underprivileged and deprived in the neighbourhood.

And that contact with the "fourth world" on their doorstep led them to begin to ask questions about their nation's role in the Third World – in Southern Africa, in Central America, in the great international financial institutions like the International Monetary Fund and the World Bank. More conflict. More resignations, departures, attempts to starve the church into submission. Complaints were sent to the hierarchy. The minister was "invited" to move. He refused.

Looking from the outside at this point, you'd say that that church was dying. Numbers were less than a quarter of their level two years earlier. Funds were so low that necessary maintenance couldn't be undertaken: the minister's salary went unpaid. Most of the "normal" churchy activities had stopped — including the contribution to denominational headquarters. It seemed to be only a matter of time before the authorities would be able to declare the church unviable, and take the necessary legal steps to close it down. Death, in a word, was imminent.

But that's the oddity. As that little group really began to live out the new quality of life it had discovered — often at great personal cost and anguish — it began slowly to attract others to it, even a few of those who had gone off in disgust at the "way things were going", as they had put it. The real turning point came, however, in another encounter with death — this time real, physical, literal death. Concerned that their government might attack Nicaragua, the church determined to send a delegation of its members to that country to see for themselves what was going on. With a struggle they raised the necessary cash, some members remortgaging their homes to do so, and six people spent a month in Nicaragua, much of it in the war zone on the northern border round Jalapa. While they were there, the guerrilla war suddenly diminished in intensity and brutality. A captured fighter admitted that his colleagues were frightened that the death of a Gringo would alienate support for their cause from the US administration. Out of that was born the Witness for Peace, one of the most striking examples of non-violent peace-making movements of this decade . . . A church that two years ago had been little more than a corporate chaplain to the arms industry had become, through risking its own institutional and physical life, a seed for peace.

It would be nice to leave the story with our heroes galloping off triumphantly into the sunset, serenaded by heavenly choirs. Life isn't like that, least of all church life. The calumny, the subtle persecution, the institutional marginalization continues. Of course. How else could either the church hierarchy or the shipyard react? But oddly membership is now at an all-time high – and income, that indicator of church vitality so loved by ecclesiastical bureaucrats the world over, is more than triple the level it reached in the most "successful" days of the church.

So what emerges from this true story? Something I suspect like this: it is only when we are ready to let our institutions die, to risk death in response to a vision – or perhaps only a glimpse – of what true life for those institutions is all about, that that true life becomes a possibility for us.

Does that correspond to your own experience in any way? Have you ever had to make that kind of choice – between letting an institution die in the hope of a rebirth, or trying, come what may, to keep it alive?

Perhaps you would like to put yourself in the shoes of the church treasurer in the story above. Income is dropping. People are leaving. There is hurt and anger and bitterness. The chairman of the Central Board of Finance writes to you, reminding you that you have not paid your church's share of central expenses; nor carried out the agreed schedule of maintenance; that things are beginning to look very bad . . . Part of you knows he's right . . . Try composing a reply . . . Once you have done that, ask yourself what changes you would make if copies were going not only to the minister of the church, but also to the Lord . . .

You may be wondering what that story had to do with the religious experience of the people of God as recorded in the Bible. Is there any evidence in that record of anything akin to what I have described — that is, a community, or rather a small remnant of a community, risking death and finding life? I believe this is so much a part of the supernatural order of things that it would be surprising indeed if one did not find it reflected in the religious experience of the Old Testament. As it turns out, there are many examples. One of the most striking comes from the period of the exile. The divided Kingdom of Israel and Judah had finally collapsed, and all the notables of Judah had been taken off into captivity in Babylon. No hardship, you might think — like an enforced holiday in Las Vegas. Many settled down comfortably enough, married into the local population and forgot all, or nearly all, about that special relationship that God Yahweh had promised his people.

A few of the captives, however, held tight to that vision, that hope that God would not abandon them — a remarkable feat in light of the fact that all the evidence pointed the other way. It must have *felt* as though God had abandoned them — totally. Institutional death looked final. The beloved Temple, perceived as God's home among his people, lay neglected and in ruins. The law which expressed the people's response to God's love for them was largely forgotten or ignored. The great cycle of feasts which celebrated the presence of God with his people was abandoned. All the institutions of Israel's religion were dying, or dead or decomposed.

And yet, after about seventy years in exile, there emerged an astonishing man who had the marvellous absurdity to say that this was not the end. We do not know his name. We know next to nothing about him. He probably came from some kind of community that had managed to hang on to the basic elements of the faith throughout the exile, and he formed around himself a group of disciples or adherents who subsequently filled out his teaching. The basic elements of that teaching are preserved in Isaiah 40—

48, chapters that are remarkable in many ways, most of all for their glowing conviction that, however tough things may look, the captives would be allowed home, that God would keep faith with his people. This is what they heard:

> Don't be afraid, Jacob, poor worm,
> Israel, puny mite.
> I will help you – it is Yahweh who speaks –
> The Holy One of Israel is your redeemer.

We cannot recapture the revolutionary potential of that oracle. It is revolutionary because it is the first time in the religious consciousness of the Old Testament that God is referred to as redeemer – *gó-él*: the relative whose responsibility it is to get you out of a mess, a kind of well-connected god-father.

So here is this poet/prophet saying, amidst the total shambles of Judah's life, that their *gó-él* has not forgotten or abandoned them – far from it. He is actually their beloved relation who will put everything right. Impossible? So it must have seemed. But as a prophet of our own day, Gerry Hughes, reminds us in the title of his most recent book: he is, after all, *A God of Surprises*. His surprises come in many shapes and sizes: they are for institutions as well as for individuals. They are, mercifully, even for the Church.

4. "Dying – and behold we live." We have reflected on three possible senses – perhaps dilute senses – in which we might have encountered that phrase as a valid description of our own experience: "lesser deaths"; the desert; and the living death and dying life of our institutions. It is time to move on and look at Paul's claim in a literal sense: in the process of death, we find life . . . but do we?

To some people that will sound a very odd question. We are conditioned to dread death, to see it as something to be avoided, delayed, repressed from thought, suppressed from conversation, and therefore almost inevitably feared, dreaded or, perhaps most deathly of all, simply ignored.

Consider, for example, the reaction of doctors and family to the news that someone has not much longer to live. Whatever the final decision about what and how much to tell the patient, the assumption is that the approach of death is unnatural, unwelcome, a worm devouring the stamens of life.

That is a twentieth-century, North Atlantic attitude. Other cultures, other times have had a healthier and, I would even say, more life-enhancing attitude to the approach of death. I was lucky enough to live in Central Africa for a time, and one of the things that most struck me there was the continuity between life and death. A sick or very old person who was not expected to live much longer saw themselves, and were seen by the rest of the village, as well advanced on a journey that would reunite them with their ancestors, without — and this I think is the point — separating them from the village. They would not, of course, be always in their hut in their present form of flesh and blood, but they would continue to be part of the village community — as the spirit of a fire or a stone or an animal or the wind. The people of the village would still acknowledge them, honour them, even feed them with ritual offerings of maize-porridge or bananas. And in village discussions about matters of great moment — the choice, say, of a new headman or chief — the opinions of generations past would be taken into careful consideration.

Superstitious rubbish? Mumbo jumbo? That is certainly what many early missionaries thought, as they tried to suppress such practices. I'm no longer so sure. Maybe, in a mythical format, the wisdom of village Africa is reminding us that the penalty of ignoring the interpenetration of past and present is precisely that we put all our emotional eggs into the basket of the present — and when the basket collapses, when the present and the past come face to face in death, we suddenly find that meaning of the present disintegrates. We therefore run away from approaching death, and encourage our doctors in the application of more and more high technology to prolong physical life at almost any cost in terms of the quality of life thus prolonged.

I was struck, then, when Sheila Mayo, the poet and artist, spoke of a friend who had just died of cancer, as having "lived beautifully with his death". It was as though, Sheila said, the approach of death had freed him not only of the obvious things like anxieties about jobs and pensions and mortgages, but, at a much deeper level, of fear and insecurity and hatred. He was now free to be himself, to know himself, to accept himself, the evil side as well as the good side, and to rejoice in finding himself alive as himself. And of course that had made it possible for him to accept others wholly and without reservation. He no longer needed to dominate them or manipulate them or do his best to like them, however much that went against the grain. He could just be open to them at the deepest level of himself. In his last weeks, for all their pain and anguish and moments of fear, anger and self-pity, he had lived beautifully. The ugliness of death's approach had been transformed into a time of great beauty.

You might like to try a simple imaginative exercise at this point, partly to let the notions of living-in-dying come home to you at a deeper level than a quick reading of the last few paragraphs is likely to achieve, and partly as a prelude to the further development of this idea in the next few pages. You have just been told that you have less than a month to live . . . On the way home from the doctor's surgery, you meet the very person whose past behaviour towards you you find it most difficult to forgive. . . . Go up to that person and tell them what you have just heard. . . . After a little time, the other person tells you that he/she has also just been to the doctor and has been told he/she can "expect to live to be a hundred" . . . What now does it mean to you "to live beautifully with your death"?

Contemplating the approach of death, the living-into-dying, is not easy, is it? It isn't easy at the individual level — but nor is it easy at the community level. Yet as Sheila Mayo's friend found as an individual, so a community sometimes finds living-into-death can be a source of freedom. Come with me to San Pedro, a dirty, dusty suburb of Lima, Peru. The people there are poor, poor beyond description. Few have jobs; most get what living they can by begging, or making sweets or grilling maize or selling lottery tickets. Few can read or write; malnutrition, dysentery and TB are endemic. Many, many children die in the first couple of years of life.

Antonio survived. At seventeen he was a natural comedian. He played the guitar, wrote songs, told stories, made people laugh. To the people of San Pedro, it would be unthinkable to have a party without Antonio being there — or a wedding, or an anniversary or a funeral. Throughout the *barrio*, he was the acknowledged entertainer who made every gathering of the people forget, however temporarily, their daily struggle for survival, their sadness and their fear. For a few hours he made them forget their squabbles, their ancient feuds, their petty jealousies and endless suspicions — for San Pedro is no stranger to the corruptibilities of human nature.

But then Antonio was taken ill, with a rare disease of the lungs. Rapidly he went downhill. Confined to his timber bed and — despite the heat of summer — covered with rags to keep him warm, he could no longer sing and joke and laugh. He could scarcely speak.

The people of the *barrio* determined to save him. He needed expensive medicine: they would raise the money. The women made dolls out of maize cobs and rags; the men went into the hills and carried home loads of wood for sale; the children hawked sweets in the smart shopping arcades. Gradually the money trickled in, often in pathetic amounts. The first tablets were bought. Antonio's condition stabilized. Efforts were redoubled. Some families pawned their meagre possessions, even their shoes . . . to no avail. Antonio died, his little hut crowded with people, friends and strangers, as many as could reach him touching him, holding him.

I spoke not long ago to a woman, a Canadian, who worked in that *barrio* of San Pedro. "It's odd," she said, "since Antonio's death, there's a new spirit in the place. The fighting's stopped. The people are together and they are beginning to know what they can do when they pull together. 'Tonio didn't die in vain."

There was nothing, nothing beautiful about 'Tonio's death. It was slow, savage, painful and premature. Yet it brought a beauty to a drab, ugly and vicious environment that even 'Tonio's songs and jokes and music could never have brought. Although he may not have lived beautifully into his death, the community of which he was part certainly did.

I wonder if that squares in any way with your experience? You might like to think of the several "communities" of which you are a member — a family? a neighbourhood? a church? a network of old friends and acquaintances built up over the years? As you think of each of those communities, you might like to form a prayer that your death will be beautiful for them . . .

It is not easy, most of us find, to *feel* the possibility of living beautifully into death. And if we don't find it very easy at the individual level, I suspect we don't find it any easier at the group or institutional level.

Not long ago, I was in Northern Namibia, in the area where the conflict between the South African Defence Force and the South West Africa People's Organization (SWAPO) is most bitter. The war ebbs and flows across the

Angola boundary, with each side melting into the bush, to reappear indistinguishable from the wretched villagers who are caught in the middle, longing for peace with dignity.

Right on the border, at the end of a road frequently mined and ambushed, lies a once great Mission station. It has been blown up by SWAPO twice and the South Africans once: now it is regularly "cleaned up", as they put it, by the SADF. We could see the tracks of the armoured personnel carriers in the sand.

Everyone has left. The bougainvillea masks the deserted class rooms. In the dispensary, drug labels peel off the shelves, and a tap drips rusty water into the autoclave. Broken windows bang in the evening breeze. Cattle wander through the central square, searching for a mouthful of grass in the thorn scrub that encroaches on the baked mud of the playground.

You find yourself looking over your shoulder, half-expecting to catch a glimpse of — a glimpse of what? You don't even know what. The atmosphere is heavy with the soft, damp smells of the African bush at sundown, but with more than that. With memories? With fears? With longing? Yes, all of that, but more still: the tension of the war within the war; the pain within the pain; the shattering din of endless fighting within the sibilance of the African sunset.

It is not wholly deserted. A Namibian priest still lives on that station. His is a precarious existence, a constant struggle for survival — survival at every level: physical, emotional, spiritual. He endures that struggle because every Sunday people come to the station. Some leave their villages before dawn — hazardous in that environment — and move stealthily through the thorn scrub and acacias for many miles, to join the tattered, scattered, battered congregation for a couple of hours of singing, reflecting, being together before God: which is the essence of worship. For two hours a week it is as though that crumbling mortuary of hope in resurrection comes alive, and the very essence of its life is flaunted in the face of all that would destroy and negate it.

By noon, everyone has gone and the silence of the bush descends again. Huge wasps drone lazily in the frangipani; water beetles scutter, all activity and little progress, across the surface of the water tanks; and vultures roost in the mahogany trees. Death — or the promise of death — has returned.

I don't know whether that is living beautifully with death. I do know that it is living in spite of death, almost in defiance of death. And I count it a great privilege to have shared, however briefly, in that paradoxical twilight of living in the midst of dying.

I count it a privilege because of the quality of life I encountered there. This was no ordinary Sunday worship service, a kind of liturgical interruption into the real business of living. This was celebration. You could tell that in the singing. I'm no musician, but even I can tell the difference between people singing with their lips, and people singing with every ounce of their being. You could tell it in the dancing — yes, the dancing. These people have little to give as offertory: but what they give, they give with an abandon that expresses itself in a singing, swaying conga that moves up to the altar in celebration of sharing what little they have which proclaims fullness of life in the midst of decay and hopelessness. Dying they are — in every sense, from individual fatality by bomb, mine or bullet, to the slow asphyxiation of a community. Dying, yes; but yet beautifully alive.

Living beautifully into death is a gift, grace. It is not everyone's lot: much death is ugly, cruel and denying of all that is valuable. And I have no easy answer, no slick assurance for those who have experienced death, and growing into death like that. Perhaps that is how Jesus experienced it in Gethsemane, in court, in guardroom-yard and on Golgotha. And that alone makes the gift of a good death the more gracious.

5. "Dying – and behold we live." The context makes it clear that St Paul was writing, if not metaphorically, still not quite literally. We have already looked at a number of metaphorical senses in which we can take his words, but now I want to take them almost certainly more literally than he meant them. For the death/life motif in Christian (as opposed to Jewish) thought does not easily divide into metaphor and fact, into symbol and reality. For the Cross was not metaphor or symbol only. It was first – both in time and in essence – fact, reality. Unlike some modern theologians, I happen to believe the same is true of the resurrection. That the resurrection has both metaphorical and symbolic meaning far beyond our usual apprehension is no doubt true and important: we have begun to explore some of that meaning already. The historical reality of the Cross has, however, to be balanced by the historical factuality of the resurrection, or we are in danger of ending up in either a highly spiritualized account of the resurrection or something that is hard to distinguish from wishful thinking.

If, then, Paul was pointing towards a key paradox of religious consciousness in this motif, it is surely not illegitimate to edge him, as it were, a little nearer the literal, and ask what sense we can make out of the claim that one day we will discover in our death, in the actual, physical process of dying, a new source of life.

For many people today such a question is either meaningless or offensive. It may be helpful, however, if we were to take forward the experience we began in the last section, when you had been told you had only one month to live . . . That month has now passed . . . Contemplate your own dying moments, not from the outside as though you were a nurse or a relative, but from the inside, from behind your own eyes . . . You are going . . . nothing can save you . . . it's time to go. . . .

I wonder what you found there? Fear? Nothingness? Peace? Relief? Perhaps a mixture of all those? Let's have a look at each of those.

I want to start with fear because that's something the Bible, and particularly the Old Testament, knows a lot about. For most people in Old Testament times, death was a miserable business. It was a time when the best you could hope for would be to go to a place of which the original meaning is "chamber" or "waiting room". It was seen as a shadowy, uninviting mode of existence – a kind of un-heated, poorly lit, dark railway waiting room on a remote branch line on a wet winter Sunday evening. The idea was that you would be left there until the Kingdom of God was finally established and then, if you were worthy, you'd be invited to the heavenly banquet; and if you weren't, you'd have a rather less attractive future.

As the orthodox Israelite of the Old Testament reflected, as you have just been doing, he would be looking forward to leaving this world to go into the uninviting waiting room. No wonder it seemed a prospect to be dreaded. Hence the Psalmist.

> . . . my life draweth nigh unto the grave, I am counted with them that go down into the pit . . . Free among the dead, like the slain that lie in the grave, whom thou rememberest no more; and they are cut off from thy hand. Thou hast laid me in the lowest pit, in darkness, in the deeps . . .
>
> (Psalm 30)

By Jesus' day, the prospects had become even less attractive. For some of his contemporaries believed that what awaited them was not so much a British Rail waiting room as permanent residence on the town tip. "Gehenna", which in some versions is translated "hell", was in fact the place outside Jerusalem where the refuse was dumped. Worse, the law required that dead animals and the corpses of executed criminals be burnt there. So there was always a smouldering mass of garbage, foul smelling, putrid and, to an orthodox Jew, utterly defiling. Try *smelling* that pall of thick smoke . . . That gives us a good idea of the way in which many of Jesus' contemporaries thought of death — as a gateway, either to a dank waiting room, or to the corporation tip.

I wonder if you ever meet people who have a similar dread of death? More likely, I suspect, you meet people, as I do, who say they have no fear of death — only fear of dying. They don't like the idea of the pain, the lack of control, the helplessness that is undeniably the experience of many of us at the hour of death. "But as for death itself," they say, "well, that'll be that . . . The end. Finish. Nothing."

They imagine, it seems, it's like close-down on the telly. The screen goes blank — and that is all there is to it: blankness.

In a way this is even worse than the old Jewish view that, however unattractive the wait, at least there is something worth waiting for. The blank-screen view means that we have even more reason to dread death, to put it off to the last possible moment, to prolong life at whatever cost in terms of the quality of the life prolonged.

Now there is no way I can "prove" that any of those pessimistic views — the waiting room, the rubbish tip or the blank screen — is wrong. In this area, as in all the important areas of faith, one can *prove* nothing. I can, however, try to share with you why I cannot subscribe to any of those views, and why I am committed to a much more optimistic view of dying.

Immediately we encounter what looks like a contradiction in terms: the reasons that prevent me from accepting either the Old Testament or any modern pessimism about death have to do with *experience*. Experience? How can that be? No one alive has experienced death, you might reply. So how can experience help us? Let me explain, in two parts.

First, let me call as a witness none other than St Paul himself. One of the most important things about Paul was that he was brought up a Pharisee, that is a very strict, very orthodox Jew. Unlike the Sadducees, who were blank-screeners, the Pharisees were waiting-room subscribers, with more than a touch of the rubbish tip for anyone whose keeping of the law was not all that it might be. That is the set of assumptions and expectations St Paul brings with him to that extraordinary encounter on the road to Damascus.

Yet twenty years later, this waiting-room/rubbish-tip believer writes some of the most beautiful, as well as some of the most polemic, passages about the afterlife in Christian literature. It's as though he has made a huge jump. And he himself is quite clear that what makes that jump inevitable is his conviction that Christ has risen from the dead. "If Christ has not risen," he says, "then our preaching is nonsense – and your faith is nonsense. Yes, indeed, and that makes us false witnesses to God." Nothing could be more central to those twenty years of life, work and suffering than that conviction that Christ has entered this new quality of life and makes it available to those who trust him – both now *and* hereafter. "If in this life only", he says, almost as an aside, "we have hope in Christ, we are of all men the most miserable."

Somehow or other, Paul has experienced the resurrection: that is, he is unshakeably convinced of its reality because of the quality of life he has discovered for himself and witnessed in the small, struggling congregations he has established in Asia Minor and Rome. That experience is so intense he can talk about it as an appearance of the unseen

Christ. He tells the Corinthians for example: "I handed on to you the fact which had been imparted to me: that Christ died . . . that he was raised . . . that he appeared to Cephas and to the Twelve . . . and to James . . . to all the apostles . . . In the end he appeared even to me . . . I had persecuted the Church of God and am therefore inferior to all other apostles – indeed not fit to be called an apostle . . . [so] all proclaim Christ was raised from the dead" (1 Corinthians 15:3–13).

So here we have a remarkable bit of autobiography. A man of unimpeachable integrity goes through an experience of the resurrection at two levels – a deep mystical experience, and direct observation of ordinary people living out their faith. Despite his rigorous training as a Pharisee – with its waiting-room and rubbish-tip expectations – he changes utterly. Further, he is deeply aware of his own failings; again and again he comes back to his past as a principal persecutor of the Church. There could be no hope in such a case for a Pharisee; he'd be straight for the rubbish tip, never mind the waiting room. Yet, despite all that, St Paul is so convinced of and attracted to what is in wait for him – and, he tells us, for us too – on the other side of death that he scarcely cares whether he is alive or dead.

I wonder whether you can *feel* that contrast – between St Paul as destined for the rubbish tip and St Paul bubblingly confident that his own experience of the risen Christ assures him of a future quality of life that enables him to mock death: "Where is your sting? Where your victory?"

To allow that to penetrate, you might like to go back to the earlier exercise. There you were, gradually slipping away – and probably encountering, so I have dared to presume, fear, anxiety and dread . . . Now let Paul come in, sit on your bed and talk to you about his own conviction that death has neither sting nor victory . . . Tell him how you feel . . . and hear what he has to say to you . . .

Paul's change from a waiting-room view of the afterlife to one of buoyant confidence in a new quality of life is striking – but it is not unique. We can find substantial numbers of people alive today who have made the same kind of jump. Nor, and this may surprise you, were all of them deeply Christian or heavily into mysticism. Just the reverse; many of them were agnostics or materialists. In so far as they thought about the question at all, many of them would have been blank-screeners. Life would come to an end – and that would be that. The screen would go blank. So what happened to convince them otherwise?

You may think I'm going to start talking about spiritualism at this point – so I want to dissociate myself very firmly from that whole area of activity. What I *am* going to talk about is the result of careful research work by doctors and psychologists into the experiences of people who have died clinically and then been resuscitated. That is to say, their "machines" ground to a halt, and, if the blank-screen view is right, the screen should have gone blank. When they were resuscitated – i.e. the machine got going again – they should have been able to remember nothing – if, that is, the blank-screeners are right.

Take the case of the Swiss architect who was driving fast through the Gotthard Pass, lost control of his car, crashed and was, so it seemed, killed. Within a very few minutes a doctor was on the scene. He gave the architect an injection of a heart stimulant, as well as mouth-to-mouth resuscitation. The architect began to breathe: his pulse picked up. His life had been saved. Severely injured, he was taken to hospital and eventually made a complete recovery.

Here was a man who had completely grown away from his childhood religious faith. A hedonistic, fast living, not very reflective person, you might expect him to be delighted to have been saved from certain, indeed actual, death. Imagine the surprise to his family and friends, when he expressed chagrin at being hauled back to life. In the few minutes he had been clinically dead, he had had the same kind of experience that has been reported again and again by people who have been brought back to life.

The architect was, much to everyone's astonishment, really gripped by that experience. He had been in a state of such tranquillity and acceptance that he found it hard to put it into words. This is what he said: "I found this state very beautiful: it was so divine, so cosmic, so natural" — hardly words, notice, that would normally have crossed his lips before the accident. He went on: "I felt so relieved — indeed liberated — and I thought, 'At last I have arrived'."

If you are a very determined blank-screener, you might think that the architect had had a hard crack on the head and as a result was hallucinating severely. Or you might point out that maybe the brain copes with death by this kind of subterfuge — a kind of grand finale before the screen does finally blank out. You *could* put either of those arguments. I personally don't find that kind of argument very convincing, given the large number of cases now reported, the consistency of the accounts — give or take a few details — and the effect it has on the people who have had such an experience.

The main point I want to make, however, is this. If we accept these accounts of near-death experiences as evidence of *anything*, and more and more doctors and psychologists are now being forced to do so, despite the blank-screen bias of modern medicine's mechanistic view of the body — then the one thing of which they are evidence is that death brings us to a *quality* of life that is far superior to anything we are likely to find in this life. Now in Christian parlance, "eternal" life is often mistakenly taken to mean unending life, or life that goes on for ever and ever — like a bicycle chain. In reality, however, this word "eternal" is about quality, about the liveliness of consciousness. And in that sense, life-out-of-death accounts are evidence — if they are evidence of anything — that death really does take us to a new quality of life that is consistent with that biblical word "eternal".

How far can we trust these accounts? I can't answer that for you. You must decide that for yourself. Yet when I find a Danish pastor, for example, saying that, having experienced utter peace and tranquillity after a massive heart attack, "coming back to life seemed agony and disappointment, and this feeling persisted for many years" – when I hear a man like that say something as strong as that, I have to take it seriously. And when that is repeated again and again, not only in Christian countries – where you could argue that it's all autosuggestion – but in India, too, with its many different religious cultures, I begin to take it as a signpost to something that I cannot ignore.

And that something seems to me very close to what St Paul was trying to describe to the Christians at Corinth. It is an assurance so strikingly different from anything that the waiting room, the rubbish tip or the blank screen can offer that I find myself echoing St Paul: "Thanks be to God who gives us this victory."

Victor Solow "died" on the operating table of a big American hospital nearly twelve years ago. He wrote afterwards that in death he had discovered a new identity, a new "I".

This new "I" was not the I that I knew, but rather a distilled essence of it, yet something vaguely familiar, something I had always known buried under a superstructure of personal fears, hopes, wants and needs. This "I" was final, unchangeable, indivisible, indestructible . . . while unique and individual as a fingerprint. "I" was, at the same time, part of some infinite, harmonious and ordered whole. I had been there before.

That seems to me a perfect description of eternal life – or, in Paul's language, of mortality clothed with immortality; of the perishable clothed with the imperishable.

Neither Victor Solow nor the Danish pastor nor the Swiss architect *prove* that Paul was right. We still have to make a leap of faith — to accept that in death we shall find eternal life; and find it as a gift . . . But then I have always found it hard to think that a God with an infinite capacity for love had nothing better in store for us than a British Rail waiting room!

6. So far we've been looking primarily at deathly situations and asking: Where is the life in them? In what senses, if any, can life be brought out of them? Suppose we now change the emphasis a bit and put the question this way: Here we perceive life in a deathly situation, but how is that life, that bit of the resurrection, to be lived out in a way that does justice to the fact of the resurrection?

It would be good to start with a further look at some biblical material. Just as we have used Old Testament stories to help us understand the religious consciousness of the people of Israel, so let's look at New Testament stories with the same objective: let's ask how they help us understand the religious consciousness of the early Church. I want to start by looking again at New Testament accounts of Christ's resurrection, especially those of St John and St Luke, for in their versions there is quite a lot of evidence — and this is reinforced by references in many of Paul's letters — that in the early Church, Easter and Pentecost were not differentiated as starkly as we have come to expect. We separate the resurrection (Easter) and the sending of the Holy Spirit (Pentecost) by six weeks, making the point that they are two different "events". It is probable that the early Church did not know so rigid a distinction; or to put it another way, the early Church associated the sending of the Holy Spirit closely with the resurrection.

For the early Church, the resurrection is a dramatic

demonstration of the *dunamis* of God – that is to say, of his dynamo, dynamite, enormous power, a power now given to his people in the person of the Holy Spirit. In contradiction to the way we have domesticated it, Easter is not about pretty-pretty bunnies and lambs and primroses and catkins, but about the explosive, driving power of God at work in his world.

Now, that takes on a special significance when we try to recapture how the early Church thought about power. For St Paul and his contemporaries seem to have thought something like this: every person, every institution, every object had an inner essence – the pigginess of a pig or the cattiness of a cat. My wife's art tutor tells her not to worry that she can't remember exactly how a tractor looks when she's trying to paint one in an art studio in the middle of Brixton. "Don't worry about whether the exhaust pipe comes out on the left or right", he says. "Catch the essence of the tractor."

It's that essence that St Paul calls the powers, those inner drives of people, communities and things – and he thought the course of events in the world was determined by these powers.

That's a very challenging idea, and put in the language of Freud, Jung or Adler, a very modern one. We are all subject to a range of inner drives – some for good, some for evil. The name of all of us is Legion. And Paul was no romantic who thought that the good would always come out on top. He knew himself well enough to have learnt that there can be no easy guarantees of that. Indeed, he seems to have *expected* the evil drives in each of us to secure the upper hand – unless we are exposed to the dynamite power of God to, as it were, blast away the bedrock from which those evil drives emanate.

Perhaps you'd care to reflect on your own experience at this point. Are you aware of that battle deep inside you – between good and evil; between the positive, constructive, life-enhancing you, and the negative, destructive, death-advancing you? Both sides are there and we need to be in touch with both — and we need to expose *both* to that dynamite power of God, to let it give energy and power to the one, and blow the other to bits. Would you like to reflect on that for as long as it takes? Acknowledge both sides, and offer them to God.

The early Church knew that this business of being caught between good and bad was true not only of individuals, but it was also true of institutions, organizations, structures, governments, empires. Just as the evil in the individual had to be confronted and opened to the dynamite power of God, in order that the individual could be transformed, enabled, energized to become what God had wanted her to be, so with institutions: they too must be confronted and opened to the releasing, liberating, transforming love of God. That strain of thinking went deep into the soul of the early Church. That is not surprising, when we reflect that for three hundred years the Church was on the defensive, sometimes bitterly persecuted, sometimes ignored, usually despised and distrusted. So the idea that the powers and principalities were in the grip of inner drives that needed transforming looked demonstrably true, indeed patently obvious, to the early Church.

Early Christians, then, felt caught in a cross-fire. On the one side were the powers of evil embodied in political institutions. On the other was the power of the risen Christ — which they experienced as a living reality in their own lives and especially at the Lord's table in the Eucharist.

They did not see their role as purely passive victims in this cross-fire — by no means. In the Book of Revelation, for example, we see a scorching, if heavily encoded, indictment of the Roman Empire under Domitian. What is most scathingly criticized, however, is not imperial materialism, lust or immorality — though each of those gets a fair airing. What is finally damnable is Roman claims to be of ultimate significance, that is, to accord the powers and principalities of Rome a status that only God can command. No wonder the Book of Revelation finishes with a great exultant shout as the Power of the resurrected Christ, the glorious lamb, finally defeats the idolatrous powers and principalities.

"Alleluia! The Lord our God, Sovereign over all, has entered on his reign! Exult and shout for joy and do him homage, for the wedding day of the Lamb has come!" (Revelation 19:6). Why not try to enter, revel in, if you like, that sense of victory. All the moral pretentiousness of a great but finally corrupt Empire has been revealed for what it is . . . the future is open: a new start can be made . . . How does *that* feel? Transpose it, if you like, to the fall of Hitler in 1945 or of Marcos in 1985 — or proleptically, to Botha in goodness knows when. Feel the sense of relief, of joy, of freedom — and of the final goodness of God.

What on earth, you may be wondering, has all this to do with me?

Come with me to the Umtali region of what was then Rhodesia. It is one of the most bitterly fought areas in a bitterly fought war. The village of Mopadzi lives a schizoid existence: by day it is controlled by the Rhodesian army; by night by the freedom fighters. Its people are trusted by neither side and terrorized by both. As if that were not enough, the notorious Selous Scouts impersonate freedom fighters, then round up and execute any who show sympathy to their cause. Already eighteen young men and five young women have been killed in this way. Four women have been gang-raped.

The village lives on its nerves. It has little else left to live on. The army has made a half-hearted attempt to make Mopadzi a "protected village", with the result that the cattle have wandered off into the bush — or, so rumour has it, into the army's commissariat. This causes great pain and offence, especially to the older men in the village, for whom cattle have an almost mystical value. The loss goes much deeper than economics, though that alone is serious enough. Jeromo Nkadzi, for example, shakes his head in sorrow and disbelief. "A village without cattle?" he asks. "What is that? How can that be? Our ancestors always had cattle. What will they think of us, their sons, that we cannot count five head between us?"

For the women, too, it is a serious matter. For how can bride-price now be paid? And what father will allow his daughter to be married if a bride-price is not forthcoming? For lack of young men and lack of cattle, the women stay at home – and wonder what the future can hold for them. . . . Some have already decided. They have "disappeared", melted across the border, and are now, one presumes, cooking for the soldiers and refugees in the base camps; doing their washing and mending and longing for the struggle to be over.

That is a longing they share with every living creature in Mopadzi. For food is short. By night the freedom fighters come and take maize, sorghum, relish – whatever they can find. One gives willingly enough, for will not this feed our own sons and daughters? But they take more than we can spare, and leave us digging the dry earth for roots or scouring the browning bush for leaves to quieten the stomach. The army will not permit us to plant our fields when the rains come. They fear the maize and sorghum will hide "terrs", as they call our sons. They prefer the fields as smooth as a sow's back so they can see who goes where. . . . So what will we eat next year?

This war is unsettling in deeper ways. No longer do the young men listen to the elders. Even the women think they can fly in the face of our traditions, and make decisions without consulting their fathers and uncles. Where will it end? It can only end in more suffering, more confusion, more misery for our people – and for our ancestors.

Rumour reaches us that the war is nearly over; that Smith is ready to talk. . . . We dare scarcely hope that this is true, that we shall be left in peace again; that we shall be free to move around our land, tend our cattle, plant our fields, enjoy our crops. Perhaps the old ways will return; then we supervised the initiation of our young men, and our wives prepared our daughters for marriage, then our ancestors were honoured, and each man could trust his neighbour; then the elders settled disputes, and we could drink our village beer in the untroubled quiet of the evening.

Perhaps, too, if Smith is ready to talk, the freedom fighters can deliver us from the bullying and humiliations of the army, the Scouts and the civil administrators. Perhaps . . . perhaps we may never have to fawn and tremble before a white man again, with his shouting and his forms and his endless, incomprehensible orders . . . Perhaps we can know the peace of our beautiful land, the peace our ancestors took for granted. Maybe we can sing our songs again, dance our dances, live like men . . . .

Not everyone in Mopadzi was Christian. Some held to the old ways; many rode two horses, offering maize porridge to the ancestors, and going to church to sing the songs of a different tune. But this was a village that the Catholics had visited for nearly a hundred years, and which had shared the common shock and outrage when the Catholic Bishop of Umtali, Donal Lamont, had been twice tried and then deported. Smith, a white man, sending away another white man? It seems incredible . . . confusing. The white priest who still comes to the village when the army allows it said the Bishop was in trouble because he protested about the way the army treated our people. Could that be the whole truth? If so, he is sharing our suffering, for no one could doubt he loves this land.

The priest says that God sees our suffering: that it grieves him and that he will deliver us. God – or the boys in the bush? We do not know. We only want the war to be over and for our land to be at peace again . . . .

Peace, of a sort, did eventually come to Mopadzi, though the old ways have never been wholly re-established. The land is, however, now cultivated, the herds have been rebuilt, the people come and go as they wish, unmolested by army, by freedom fighters or by white administrators. To many people it seems as though one terrible aberration from the normal tenor of life has passed and normality has returned . . . .

But not to everyone. If you go to Mopadzi today you will find a few people who see both the end of the war and the end of legalized racism as God acting in history to set his people free. Perhaps that is a language they have been taught – by the radical priests in the diocese, or the young men returning from the ZANU bases. Perhaps, too, it reflects something deeper: an acknowledgement that life may, by the grace of God, be brought out of death. Certainly the last time I was in Mopadzi, one of the elders took me to the edge of the village and pointed to the bush. Although the rains had not yet begun, the drab, burnt browns were splashed with yellows, reds and brilliant greens as flowers and trees burst into bloom despite the dust-dry soil.

"You see," said the elder, "God brings life to the dead bush. So he brought us back to life, even though in many ways we are still as withered as the bush. I want my people to come alive again, as the bush is coming alive . . . That is what I want. That is what we all want . . . We ask God to give us that before anything . . . .

Despite everything – the past and the ambiguities of both present and future – he *wanted* to live the resurrection. Perhaps he could see what that meant only dimly. His was a simple, wavering faith, but a faith that could intuit that what was happening around him – and what he wanted to happen for his people – had something to do with the heart of the faith the missionaries had brought. He realized, too, that coming to life again after the trauma of war and the long leaching of a racist state, demanded a response from the villagers. For them to live the resurrection was both gift and effort, grace and will-power.

That seems to me always to be the nature of the resurrections we experience in this life. God may give them; but we have to take them. God cannot, as it were, live our resurrections for us. He can – and does – give us the opportunity and the spiritual resources: but it is up to us whether or not we then live out the possibilities we are given. It is always left open to us to remain in our deaths. Life is offered to us; not forced upon us.

If that is true at the individual level – in, for example, our closer relationships – it is no less true surely in our social and political deaths and resurrections. Like the people of Mopadzi, we may find God acting in history to open new opportunities of freedom and growth. We, however, have to take responsibility for what we make of those opportunities. It is that which gives political creativity its arc of ultimate significance.

Before we move to another example, perhaps you would care to reflect on the story and the last two paragraphs. Where in your life do you experience the tension between the grace of God giving resurrection and your response of commitment, effort and courage? . . . You might like to reflect on that from three perspectives – your personal relationships; the life of your immediate community; and the life of your nation. . . . Where is God offering the possibility of new freedom and what are you doing about it? . . .

My last example was about resurrection being offered to those who had been caught in the middle of a dirty war. To be true to the Revelation of St John the Divine, however, we need an example of someone or some people finding resurrection, or rather appropriating resurrection, in the process of taking sides in the great cosmic battle described by St John. In its pure form we cannot find that. No human enterprise is so free of ambiguity and compromise that it can be taken as an unequivocal proxy for the cause of Christ. Yet sometimes we are, or feel we are, on the fringe of that battle. . . . The peace people, the Greens, the gays, the feminists, the blacks, the job-marchers are all people in our own society who know they are engaged on a struggle that has a wider dimension than the parochial or the self-interested.

So did Brother Thomas, as I shall call him. He worked in a slum parish in a large industrial city, an area so run-down and demoralized that living conditions are among the worst in England. A housing charity bought a terrace of dilapidated houses, intending to convert them, modernize them and make them available at low rents to homeless families. (Existing tenants would have prior claim, but the charity reckoned they would have sixty-five "new" flats available.) Brother Thomas was contacted to help identify homeless families in greatest need and, with much effort, he and local community leaders began to produce a list of sixty-five families. It was at this point that the charity received a letter from the Housing Department, saying that as planning permission had had to be given for the renovation, the Housing Department would choose tenants for thirty of the sixty-five new flats. Both the officers of the charity and Brother Thomas were surprised at this development, but assumed that the Housing Department would allocate the flats to the most neeedy. As work on the flats neared completion, however, Brother Thomas was enraged to discover that twenty-eight of the thirty had been allocated to employees of the Housing Department.

"It was a body blow to the people here", said Thomas later. "It meant that about a hundred and fifty people who could have had decent houses would have to remain where they were – some, travellers, in damp caravans on odd bits of waste ground; some in warehouses; some in old tenements that should have been pulled down years ago. But the odd thing was that it stirred people – even those who were not directly involved . . . For years we've been trying to get this community together, to do such simple things as nominate representatives to the Police Liaison Committee or organize a community festival. We'd never got anywhere. It was like bashing your head on a feather mattress.

"Then, when this housing thing blew up, it was as though people suddenly saw the point; as though there was something they could all relate to. Within two weeks of the Housing people's list appearing, they had organized a round-the-clock picket on the new flats. The Housing Department sent the police in – and that clinched it. Nothing would shift those people now. A week later they were not only picketing the flats; they were holding a permanent vigil outside the offices of the Housing Department. And it wasn't just the people who might have thought they were being elbowed out by the Housing Department's nominees. It was everyone – even the local GP took his turn.

"And the funny thing was that as the people became more determined, so they became more open to us. People who had abused us for years suddenly turned round and welcomed us. We'd even been invited to celebrate Mass ouside the Housing Department for the picket . . . Pity, that . . . The Housing Department capitulated thirty-six hours before our Mass . . ."

Read what you will into that story. Brother Thomas sees it as a community being touched with resurrection life – and discovering what it means to come alive only in the confrontation with great injustice.

In many ways Brother Thomas' story always reminds me of the final defiant utterance of the Christian Institute in South Africa, banned in 1977. One of the last issues of the Institute's journal, *Pro Veritate*, had this to say:

Christians who prophesy only doom must realize they are not speaking with a Jesus voice. . . . God is busy with his programme. The strategy of God is at work in our history, and it is our task to find and follow his purposes. This is what the Christian faith is about.

"God is busy with his programme" in the United Kingdom, from Brixton to Birmingham and Ballachulish. And that programme is a resurrection programme that does justice to the transformation of the quality of life God wants for his people. "It is our task to find and follow his purpose." Some task — but one a lot of Christians are already deeply engaged in. Some find it in the peace movement. Some in the inner cities. Some in the ecology movement. Some through Amnesty International or the World Development Movement. Some in the gentle nourishment of those in the front line. Wherever they are, they will tell you, far better than I, that they have experienced the truth of that crazy Christian assertion: dying — and behold we live!

Summary of Exercises

1. What moments of lesser death have you experienced? How did it feel?

2. Transpose Abram's call into your own terms and meditate on the "leave . . . and I will" contrast.

3. Remember meditatively your own desert.

4. Who/what are your own Baalim? (See p. 49).

5. What are your real feelings about the institutional Church?

6. As church treasurer under financial pressure from denominational headquarters, give an account of your stewardship — first to the denominational finance office and then, separately, to Christ.

7. What does it mean to you to live beautifully with your death? (See pp. 60–64).

8. Form a prayer that your death may be beautiful for the several communities of which you are a part (p. 64).

9. Contemplate your own dying moments . . . tell Paul how you feel about it . . . listen to his response.

10. Look at the positive and negative parts of your make-up and invite God to work on each (p. 69).

11. Celebrate the goodness of God acting in history as a rotten State is finally swept away (p. 76).

12. Where in your life do you experience the tension between the grace of God giving resurrection and your response of commitment, effort and courage? Reflect on this from three perspectives: your personal relationships, your community and your nation.

5.

Disciplined By Suffering But Not Done To Death

Suffering does to death. We need to be clear about that in case we get swept away by romanticism about suffering that flies in the face of most people's experience. Whether physical, mental, emotional or spiritual, the hurts of suffering have to be named for what they are — destructive, diminishing, demoralizing and fearful. Just as we Christians are apt to get starry-eyed about poverty — until we know what it is to have to count the minutes of a one-bar heater in the depth of winter — so we get immuned to the reality of suffering — until we are in intensive care or on the analyst's couch. A priest-friend who has just had a very unpleasant operation said when I visited him in hospital: "I shan't talk so glibly of weakness again. I know what it is now — and that is body-knowledge." Perhaps only body-knowledge in the end will suffice to cure us of our over-intellectualization of concepts that lie near the heart of the Gospel. And that suffering certainly does.

It is not only us as individuals who are done to death by suffering. The same is true of communities and nations. I remember the surprise and anguish I experienced when I visited Crossroads in Cape Town in 1983, before, that is, it had exploded but at a time when it had already attracted international attention as the residents resisted eviction or forcible resettlement at the new — but distant, ill-provided and heavily controlled — township of Khayelitsha. In retrospect, I'm not sure what I expected to find — a palpable spirit of co-operation and quiet determination? A mutuality and solidarity that held the community together despite the poverty and the harassment? A simple nobility that refused to be broken by economic and political deprivation? Unconsciously perhaps all of those, with a little home-grown romanticism thrown in.

The reality was quite different. Worse than the evident poverty and physical hardship – and in my judgement they had been under-reported rather than exaggerated – worse was the sense of a group of suffering people whose very suffering prevented them from becoming a community. Exploitation; racketeering; protection rackets; informing (which was often misinforming); looting and burning and beating by privately-run gangs of thugs; theft; misappropriation of collective funds; drunkenness and prostitution on a grand, but at the same time squalid, scale – all this and more made the confrontation with the authorities over the proposed move to Khayelitsha relatively minor burden in the daily lives of the residents. What had been represented as the central issue in the consciousness of some of the most oppressed people on God's earth turned out not to be unimportant or insignificant, but more beyond emotional comprehension, in a situation that had simply collapsed as a viable way of living at anything more than a survival level. It is, of course, a matter of debate about how far the problems of Crossroads stem directly from the economic and political oppression of the people; how far from the breakdown of cultural norms as a result of rapid urbanization; and how far from human failings. There is no way of finally knowing that, and people inevitably bring their own ideological baggage to such a judgement. What is clear is that in an environment as hellish as Crossroads, suffering does to death. It kills community. It kills hope. It kills mutuality. And in 1986 it made a quantum leap in the scale on which it kills people.

Suffering kills ideals. We have all seen that at the personal level: the man in pain becomes self-centred, irritable and inconsiderate. The heart-broken woman can see no one else's grief but her own. Suffering suffocates idealism at the community or national level too. Many of us saw the overthrow of Somoza in Nicaragua not only as a desirable political change but as God acting in history in the spirit of the Magnificat. Here indeed the rich were being sent empty away (if only as far as Miami!), and the hungry were being filled with the good things of a peasant's life – beans, maize and eggs.

The unlikely combination of Marxist guerrilla leaders and "radical" priests might be able, it seemed, to transform a small but fertile country from a personal fiefdom marked by one of the highest infant mortality and illiteracy rates on the continent, to a society where everyone would have enough and no-one would flaunt excess. The early signs were encouraging. Illiteracy was tackled at a rate that the experts had said was impossible. Infant mortality fell in the face of a programme of primary health care that made Nicaragua the darling of UNICEF and the World Health Organization. Land reform was implemented so that peasants could form co-operatives, and many showed a shrewdness and dedication in bringing their land into production that astonished international observers. Above all, there was a sense of a just purpose, a meaningfulness and a creativity that made the short flight from San Salvador to Managua – from "free" El Salvador to "communist" Nicaragua, in the language of the right-wing gutters further north – a journey that most people found one of the most exciting of their lives. Halcyon days . . . .

The ensuing five years brought trade embargoes; constant harassment by land, air and sea; disinformation in the world's media on a scale that many of us still find literally incredible; and the steady, relentless strangulation of an attempt, sometimes clumsy, sometimes foolish, to translate the Magnificat into political reality.

The suffering thus implied is not only the deaths of innocent people along the Honduran border nor the economic dislocation that puts beans and maize again beyond the certain grasp of the most disadvantaged families. The most painful suffering, and one freely articulated in the most humble *barrios*, is the sense of hurt and outrage at being denied the possibility of creating a just society, or, at the very least, a society in which the basic needs of everyone would take priority over the fancies of the few.

It is this frustration, I think, that explains the increasingly strident militarism of Nicaraguan society. Threatened by the Contras (the "counter-revolutionaries", many of them former cronies or employees of Somoza), it was inevitable that Nicaraguans would defend themselves. But I observe something more than that: almost a glorification of armed struggle, the absolutization of military prowess. From graffiti to popular songs, to allocation of desperately scarce financial resources, one sees a national fixation with gun-power that is nearly as far removed from the spirit of the Magnificat as are the Contras themselves. However understandable in human and political terms that may be, the result is that the original ideals – or at least one strand in those ideals – has not just been lost: it has been turned inside out.

Before we look at what might lie behind this, it might be helpful to spend a little time reflecting on your own experience of suffering; suffering, that is, that does to death. You might like to start by looking at your own suffering – physical, emotional, spiritual. Recall the horror of the suffering. Don't gild it. Face it as honestly as you dare, neither exaggerating it ("Some Christians think they are experiencing the Cross when they have a headache", a senior Cambridge cleric complained) nor romanticizing it. . . . Then ask yourself, "What has that suffering done to death in me?" The answer will probably be a mixture of things, but for the moment I'd like you to concentrate on the good, or potentially good, things that have been killed by that experience of suffering . . . a relationship? your inner tranquillity? your faith? your capacity to respond to the needs of others?

Then look at your local community. Is there any sense in which that has suffered – through a local disaster? or high unemployment? or a sudden deterioration in the environment? or the gradual leaching away of its most gifted or vigorous members? What has that killed in the community? . . .

Then you might like to ask the same question of your church. In what senses has that suffered? . . . a loss of leadership? internal strife? slow asphyxiation? the wrong kind of success? And what has been killed? . . .

Suffering does to death. And it does to death the wrong things in the wrong people. It kills love and gentleness and openness in individuals, often the very individuals who prize and are seeking to enlarge those virtues. And it kills energy, joy and creativity in communities, even in God's own community, the Church.

Now I know that is only half the story. Sometimes suffering transforms people, institutions, communities. The history of the Church is full of such, a fact that led Eric Abbott to coin the remarkable aphorism: "In His army, only the wounded can serve." The theme of the wounded healer is older than the Cross itself – and wider than the Christian faith. All that may be granted and properly honoured. It does not, however, remove the deathliness of suffering: it merely highlights the mystery of life sometimes brought out of that death.

For the domain of suffering is death. That is to say, suffering is the denial of the fullness of life that God gives his people. Or, to use an unfashionable language, suffering is of the devil. It is the work of the devil. It is the territory of the unredeemed powers and principalities, whose activity is dis-integration, the denial of wholeness and therefore of holiness.

In this sense, Christ's ministry on earth has at its centre a series of encounters with the powers of dis-integration. The most explicit is the curing of Legion, the very symbol both of suffering (its outward manifestations, notice, brought upon himself as he gashes his own flesh) and of dis-integration: "We are many." The same theme, however, runs in nearly all the healing stories, where Christ is represented as confronting and overcoming the "evil spirits" that cause illness, whether physical or psychological. The coming of the Kingdom of God is thus proclaimed in the overthrow of the powers that divide, destroy and diminish the people of God.

On this account, then, suffering is the momentum, as it were, of the dynamic of death that Christ proclaims is to be reversed. Its reversal is itself a sign of the breaking in of the Kingdom. When the destructive power of suffering is checked, *there* is the Kingdom of God.

Two observations of great importance then follow. First, when St Paul writes "disciplined by suffering, we are not done to death", he is not making a pious comment on his ability to withstand the suffering he has earlier catalogued. He is saying that the power of suffering has already been broken and *therefore* his life and ministry is to be seen as part of the breaking-in of the Kingdom of God. He is thus identifying himself with the life of Christ. This is consistent with his earlier claim to be judged by "innocence of . . . behaviour; by gifts of the Holy Spirit; by sincere love; by declaring the truth; by the power of God . . ." It is also, of course, consistent with the polemic of the whole of this part of the letter. For if his ministry is really at one with the Kingdom of God, how can his Corinthian critics resist it?

Second, we need to pause for a moment on the word "disciplined". In the light of all that we have said about suffering being the work of the devil, how can Paul use of it a positive word like "disciplined"? (I say positive, not because I like the authoritarian flavour of discipline as in the military or law-and-order senses, but because in the Greek, the meaning is much nearer that of teacher or instructor. Discipline in this sense is a method by which we learn things that redound to our own good.)

St Paul is disciplined by suffering, taught by suffering, precisely because its destructive power is reversed, and instead of being "done to death", he and his friends incorporate truth, patience, kindliness and the gifts of the Spirit. In other words, in the context of the coming of the Kingdom, suffering can be used redemptively. It can become a teacher that enlarges and purifies, instead of diminishing and corrupting.

From that follows a third point of great significance. Earlier in this meditation, we thought of suffering in our own lives and in the lives of communities of which we are a part. As we recalled that suffering, we dwelt primarily on the deathly nature of suffering. Yet at the back of our minds, so I suppose, there lay the other half of the truth: that sometimes, for ourselves, for others we know well and even for whole communities, suffering has indeed been redemptive. It has set us free from preoccupation with self. It has made us broaden our horizons. It has given us insight into the condition of others . . . .

Will you test that now against your own experience? Go over the material you looked at earlier in this meditation and ask yourself what positive things came out of it. Where can you see the purposes of God being worked out through that suffering? In what senses, if any, was that episode – or chronic condition – of suffering a benevolent teacher that led you into a deeper understanding of yourself and your relations with the loving purposes of God? . . . And ask the same questions of your community and your church.

What I hope you will glimpse in this is that when suffering does acquire a redemptive edge, *that* is the Kingdom of God breaking in around you and your family, your friends and your community. It is at that point that the Kingdom of God is among you, for the power of suffering to kill and destroy has been overcome and, miraculously as well as paradoxically, life has been brought out of the domain of death.

"But why", we ask, "does it happen for some people and not for others? Why does this sick person become introverted, selfish and bitchy; while that one is able to transcend the pain and find a new dimension to her life?" We could ask the same question of communities, secular or religious. Why is this community destroyed by some painful shock, while that one uses it as material for growth?

I have no answer to that question. It is part of the mystery of grace, and is no more easily answered than why God chose the Jews as the people of redemption; or why he chooses Joe Bloggs to be the recipient of the gift of faith but not Mary Smith. In other words, that "ability" to transcend suffering is not an ability that we can acquire by dint of hard work or moral excellence. Rather, it is gift, pure givenness — which we may certainly ask for, whether for ourselves or others; and with which we shall certainly need to co-operate if it is to be a gift well received. Above all, it is a gift for which we can be profoundly and joyfully thankful. For it means that even in our weakness, even — indeed, especially — at our low points, God can proclaim through us his endless graciousness by surrounding us with signs of the bursting in of his Kingdom.

That, it seems to me, is the true nature of the discipline of suffering that does not do to death. It is the joyful teaching that the destructive power of the Evil One has been, and is now being, overcome by pure grace.

Perhaps you would care to conclude this meditation by thanking God for that grace — at work all around you. Go back to the people or groups or events you identified earlier as those who are not done to death by their suffering. . . . Take each and glorify God for what he is doing with them and through them. . . . You may wish to use as a mantra or coda, the words of someone who grappled with these issues millennia ago and, in the terms of contemporary religious consciousness, came to a strikingly similar conclusion:

> Then Job answered the Lord:
>> I know that thou canst do all things
>> and that no purpose is beyond thee.
>> But I have spoken of great things which
>>> I have not understood,
>> things too wonderful for me to know.
>> I knew of thee then only by report,
>> but now I see thee with my own eyes.
>> Therefore I melt away;
>> I repent in dust and ashes.   (Job 42:1–6; NEB)

Summary of Exercises

1. Face your own experience of suffering. What has that suffering done to death in you? Ask the same question of your community . . . and your Church . . . .

2. . . . And what has suffering brought alive in you, your community and your church?

3. Take each person or group or event where you see the deathly power of suffering being overcome, and give thanks for it as a sign of the coming of the Kingdom.

6.

In Our Sorrows, We Have Always Cause For Joy

There is a brand of Christianity that denies or defies the sorrows of life. The great American scholar and spiritual guide, Martin Marty, calls it a "summery spirituality" and describes it like this: "A person can best display the fulfilled soul by jumping up and down. The songs of faith, say the instructions, have to shout the language of abundance and life. The rites with which one passes through the stages of life have to represent emotionally violent turns from the old self to the born-again new being. Never look back – or within – is the counsel. The ways of the Lord are no longer mysterious. People reduce them through easy explanations. They burst with shadowless joy with the heart. Enjoy these ways . . . ."

This "summery spirituality", where all is light and sunshine and fruitfulness, may have its place, but its place is in a scheme of things that takes proper account of the passing of the seasons. In our northern latitudes, summer is short, no more than four months at best – and that means that the harsher, colder, more demanding climate of the other eight months is the more general experience.

I'm told that many perennial plants need the harshness of winter as much as they need the softness of summer. Certainly a friend and neighbour in Zambia, who did much pioneering work in introducing temperate plants to Zambia's near-ideal climate, found that many fruit trees needed an artificial winter, when they could die back and rest, if they were to be fruitful. Perpetual summer sapped their strength and vitality.

In Our Sorrows, We Have Always Cause For Joy

As so often, there is a striking parallelism, I believe, between the natural world and the world of the spirit. A spirituality that refuses to acknowledge the winter of the heart, the great sorrowfulness of human experience, is not only refusing to take seriously the life that people actually lead: it is in danger of encouraging too much leaf and too little fruit.

In that sense, our "sorrows" are not *only* negative, destructive and painful. Yes, they are those things: it would be as misleading as it would be dangerous to deny that. That is not, however, all they are. They are also the necessary period of die-back, perhaps the continuing process of die-back, which is a precondition of fruitfulness.

It is therefore important to be in touch with our sorrows, to recognize them, to honour them even. So often we imagine there is virtue in pretending they don't exist. We treat them as Victorian *grandes dames* treated the wayward son, labelling him "black sheep" and dispatching him to the colonies so that he could be forgotten or ignored until he returned reformed, rich and famous. There is reason for that, of course. Having him around is painful, not least to the family pride.

In the same way, living in the presence of our sorrows is always painful, and one of the bits of us that is hurt most of all is our pride. I hate to acknowledge that I cannot love my mother; that I despise my brother; that I have made a mess of my career or my marriage. How much more comfortable to my self-esteem to push all those feelings away, to pretend to myself and everyone else that everything in the garden is lovely, that summer will last for ever.

Living in the presence of our sorrows requires courage. It is not something that can be done quickly or easily. Nor is it something to be attempted unless we are ready to put in the work that will be required to discover the joyful side of the sorrow. I make those caveats before inviting you to spend a little time in bringing to mind your own sorrows;

gently lifting them out of that mental limbo to which you may have consigned them, and honouring them as part of your own spiritual landscape.

There are many ways of doing this, and what matters is that you are faithful to your own experience rather than to any checklist or procedure that I might suggest. If nothing comes to you as you reflect on your own experience, you may like to try asking yourself what it is that leaves you sad, irritated, "out of sorts", discomposed or unhappy? A relationship that won't heal? a part of your life that you feel defensive about? a memory that you instinctively bury as soon as it surfaces? a sense of failure or inferiority or rejection? . . . Perhaps nothing comes alive for you now. So wait until you do feel angry or ill at ease with yourself, and then take a little time to identify what lies behind it. Once you have identified it, bring it into the open, sit it down in the sun and have a good, even respectful, look at it. Sorrows are for honouring, not for burial.

To some people, all this honouring of sorrows may seem morbid or counter-productive. Isn't it better, they might well ask, to let sleeping dogs lie? If I can repress my resentments, my hatreds, my distorted sexuality, my psychic pain of whatever origin, why not enjoy the peace that repression gives me?

That reaction is natural, but, as I believe, mistaken. It is not only bad psychology: practically every school of psychotherapy encourages us to be aware of what causes us pain, if only because we need for more creative purposes the energy that otherwise goes into the process of repression itself. It is also, I believe, bad religion because it cuts us off from one whole area of identification with Christ. For Christ almost certainly identified closely with that strange, allusive figure that appears in a number of poems in the later chapters of our book of Isaiah, poems probably collected by a group or school of prophets and mystics in the sixth century BC and usually called the Songs of the Suffering Servant.

"A man of sorrows, acquainted with grief . . ." The

Suffering Servant knows little of summery spirituality. "Stricken", "afflicted", "wounded", his sorrows are physical and immediate; but they are also psychic, spiritual. He knows his grief. He is acquainted with it as a familiar friend. He lives in its presence.

Jesus lived the same way. Although I am often struck by his sense of fun, his humorousness, his ability to live life to its fullest, he was not unacquainted with grief. He lived in the presence of his sorrows — none more than the continuous sorrow of rejection by the ecclesiastical establishment of his day.

The very people who should have rejoiced to hear that the Kingdom of God had come among them sniped and snarled, plotted and planned to get rid of him who offered them such threateningly good news. For Jesus their reaction was not (only?) personally painful. What grieved him was the impact the defensive religiosity of the establishment had on the poor, the less privileged, the ordinary people who found the burdens of the Law too much to bear. More than that, he seems to have been conscious of the historical as well as the human cost of the rejection of his ministry. He weeps over Jerusalem because he is aware of the inevitability of its destruction. Unable to change, unable to respond to the opportunity he offers it, its doom is sealed. There is no trace of *Schadenfreude* or vengeance in his grief: he knows too well the implications of a punitive raid by an imperial army keen to restore its image. If only . . . if only. . . . But the realities are clear. And Jesus carries them with him to his death.

I think it is important to rediscover this continual ache that Jesus knew, because we so often imagine that his ministry was unaffected by sorrows until it became clear that the leading Jews would be satisfied with nothing less than his death. When we can see him as a man of sorrows, acquainted with grief throughout his ministry, we can live in the presence of our own sorrows more hopefully. We discover that we do not need the assurances — whether true or false — of a summery spirituality: we can live with the harshness of winter in the hope of its ultimate passing.

Certainly that seems to have been St Paul's own experience. "In distress, hardships and dire straits; flogged, imprisoned, mobbed; overworked, sleepless, starving . . ." And on top of all that, his "infirmity of the flesh" as a constant reminder of his physical weakness, a sorrow that he can never forget, never repress. Yet what he discovers in the midst of this is not just hope — hope, that is, in the popular sense of some future relief or improvement. "In our sorrows", he writes, "we have always cause for joy." Living in the presence of his sorrows, he exults in the fact that they finally define neither the present nor the future.

How can that be? The key lies in his conviction, stated a few verses earlier, that in Christ we are "made one with the goodness of God himself"; we "have received the grace of God." What do those phrases really mean as we come, so painfully and humiliatingly, to live in the presence of our own sorrows? How do they provide "cause for joy"?

We need to enter a little more fully into St Paul's understanding of human personality and its relationship to the whole created order. We tend to think of a two-dimensional world: there are human beings as it were "on earth", and there is God (plus angels perhaps) "in heaven". We tend to be rather vague about how these interact, though most of us would see the sacraments as a particular means of interaction. To St Paul this would have seemed a bare and inadequate account. For him there was a whole range of "principalities and powers", "authorities" and "dominions" that separate humanity from God. Some of those intermediate powers are redeemed and therefore reconciled to God; others are demonic, constantly in conflict with God. Whether angelic or demonic, however, they interact with the human world, through persons (and their personalities) as well as through their institutions, politics, histories and structures.

St Paul thus sees us as caught up in the great cosmic battle between God and Satan, good and evil. Unless we are "in Christ" – that is, made part of him by dying and rising with him through the symbolism of baptism – we are at the mercy of the cosmic forces engaged in this battle. We can be overwhelmed, almost literally taken-over, by the demons and demi-gods who enslave us. They are the cosmic forces of our sorrows. Or, to put it the other way round, our sorrows are the incarnation of these demons, ever willing to enslave and destroy us. Whether our sorrows be our physical pain; our personal failings or weakness of character; our relationship to others; or un-transcended memories of trauma or sadness – whatever they may be, they are the stuff, the embodiment, of forces of evil that have an existence independent of our particular experience of them.

This may sound far-fetched or superstitious to us, brought up in a popular scientism with its own rules and language. Yet the striking thing is that many great modern thinkers, from Marx to Jung to van der Post, hint at the need to re-invent, if not demi-gods at least orders of being that transcend the purely individual or institutional. For all his materialism, Marx wants to talk about the "essence" of humanity, and the "spirit" of capitalism. Jung has to invent the idea of the "collective unsconscious" to explain how we relate to each other at a level deeper than words or normal intercourse. Laurens van der Post, following Jung in so many things, sees supposedly primitive peoples as being in touch with energies and powers that our allegedly advanced culture ignores, neglects or has forgotten.

Whether or not you find any of that style of thinking resonates with your own experience, the key thing is to see that for St Paul being "in Christ" enables us to share in his victory over the demonic world. For Christ's resurrection, St Paul says, is final proof that these demons have indeed been defeated. They have been "put down". They can no longer aspire to reign supreme, though those who cut themselves off from Christ may still be wholly subject to their authority. For they are not yet finally eliminated. Indeed, if we are not on our guard, they can still take us captive, still generate new sorrows. Like weeds, they still grow with the wheat, though their doom is sealed.

When Paul writes of his conviction that in Christ we are "made one with the goodness of God himself", he is expressing his confidence that Christ's death and resurrection guarantees us victory over the demons, uniting us with their opposite, the power of God's goodness. That is the grace of God: both his graciousness in offering us that possibility; and his power to make that possibility real.

No wonder he can say that in his sorrows, he always has cause for joy. The sorrows are real, enduring and painful. Like weeds, they are still-existing manifestations of the powers of evil. As such, they have to be recognized for what they are; named; or, as our argot has it, fingered. But they point beyond themselves. They do not define the limits of human experience or the end of human possibilities: for they are already defeated, rendered impotent as the parameters within which life must be lived. The limits of human potential are defined only by union with the goodness of God himself.

Rhetoric — or reality? There is no religious question more basic. Is the world finally controlled by evil — or by good? Or are we no more than flotsam and jetsam washed about in the rip-tide of those opposing forces, waiting to be swept in the direction of the dominant force?

That is an invitation to more reflection on your own experience. Again, this is not easy or quick. It is something you may need to come back to again and again, for it is fundamental. The questions on which you may want to hang your reflection could be these: as I look back on my life, where have I been aware of this cosmic struggle — in myself? in social and political life? in the life of the

Church? in ideas, ideals and cultures? In what ways have I been aware, however dimly, of Christ's victory? Where have I glimpsed what it means to be in union with the goodness of God — in my own life? in the lives of others? Have I experienced that as the grace of God? . . .

If you find that rather a mouthful, you may find it less hard to chew if you concentrate initially on one major turning point of your life, ideally a particular decision that changed the range of opportunities — for better or worse, or even both — open to you. As you recall the process of making that decision, what was going on . . . ? In you . . . ? But also in the whole spiritual environment in which you are set? Was the decision only a matter of rational analysis plus glandular chemistry . . . ? or were there more "subterranean" influences that predisposed you, guided you, one might even say, in the direction you took . . . ? You may not have been aware of them at the time, but are you aware of them as you look back . . . ? Does that give any kind of signpost to Christ's victory?

Two final comments. Living in the presence of our sorrows should increase rather than diminish our joy, but it will be winter-hardened joy. And, secondly, that should mean it will be more fruitful. For a proper living-through of the sorrow/joy paradox delivers us from an over-concern with our own sorrows. Indeed it sets us free from their destructive power, allowing us to put more time and energy at the service of our neighbour. And that, too, is cause for joy.

Summary of Exercises

1. Honour our own sorrows.

2. Honour Jesus' sorrows.

3. Where have you been aware of the cosmic struggle – in yourself? in social and political life? in the life of the Church? in ideas, ideals and cultural norms?

4. How have you been aware of Christ's victory in that struggle? (pp. 101–2)

5. Where have you glimpsed what it means to be in union with the goodness of God? in your own life? in the lives of others?

6. How far have you experienced that as the grace of God? (p. 103)

7.

Poor Ourselves,
We Bring Wealth To Many

A good way into the religious consciousness of any age lies in its art. Its artists tell us much about how that age sees mankind, its problems, its opportunities, its achievements, its fears and its hopes. Compare, for example, the finely balanced, exquisitely proportioned, intensely rational sculpture of classical Greece with, to take an extreme example, the deeply disturbed and turbulent world of the Dadaists of the 1920s. And if we want to know about images of God, it is well to ask the artists.

Perhaps one of the odd things about western Christianity is that if we look at artists' images of God from the Middle Ages to the last century (when artists largely lost interest in God, though not necessarily in religion), what is likely to strike us is that God is nearly always represented as a great authority figure. In the Middle Ages he is a heavenly baron, or a king, or a judge. Fighting, ruling, condemning to death seem to be his major occupations. Perhaps one of the best known of the post-medieval pictures of God is by William Blake. Eyes flashing, arm outstretched, finger pointing, God is leaning out of a thunder cloud, surrounded by lightning, issuing a terrible command. Here is Authority personified, demanding obedience, brooking no delay or temporization, ready to punish the least deviation from his commands with fearful severity.

That is the God who became the God of Empire, whether Spanish, Portuguese or British. However eloquently missionaries spoke of a compassionate, suffering Christ, the God of the missionizing Powers was experienced as a God of the corvée, forced labour, of forcible eviction from ancestral land, of harsh taxation, of arbitrary power over life and death, of unquestioning obedience. This was a God of great power and wealth, leaving the Incas, the Zulus, the Bengalis and the Chitralis broken and impoverished people. "Poor ourselves, we bring wealth to many" must have sounded odd in the ears of such people, especially coming from the lips of those who, whatever the legal and constitutional niceties, seemed indistinguishable from the army officers, civilian administrators and commercial agents of this Imperial God. Perhaps it still does.

There is, I believe, a part of us that still wants a God like that. We no longer need him, of course, as an accoutrement to our colonial ambitions – though a moment's reflection on the uncomfortable synergy between official religion and military adventurism at the time of the Falklands disaster will remind us not to be too optimistic that we have wholly outgrown the need for a Baron God who will lead us successfully into battle. We want a God who dominates, who robs us of choice, who spares us the agony of taking responsibility for our own lives. Under his command, we can remain immature and dependent, serfs and villeins scurrying unthinkingly to do our Master's bidding, however outrageous and immoral that may be.

Against this background I found a novel by the Japanese author Shusaku Endo particularly striking. In *Silence* Endo, himself a Catholic who found the western imperial God deeply at odds with his own Japanese culture, tells how a Jesuit priest, Rodrigues, goes to Japan in the seventeenth century to discover why his former mentor had renounced his Christian faith. Rodrigues is zealous, tough, a hardened soldier for Christ – and yet in his search finds the Christ he has been trained to follow loyally is silent. At the end of the novel, Rodrigues is captured, imprisoned and finally ordered to follow his mentor's example and renounce his faith. To symbolize his final abandonment of Christ, he is instructed to grind an icon in the mud under his foot. He hesitates — and is told that so long as he delays Christian prisoners will be tortured. In an agony of indecision, he suddenly hears the long-silent Christ speak to him. "Trample! Trample my face!", says the filthy icon. "It is to be trampled on by you that I am here."

Nothing could better capture the rejection by the book's author of the Imperial God. It is only when the icon is lying in the mud, shorn of all glory and power and dignity, that he can allow it to speak, "a forsaken Christ to a forsaken man; a suffering Christ to a suffering man; a Christ who had been very near apostasy to a man about to apostasize. Only such a Christ could bring a word of acceptance, peace and hope in such a time to such a man." And it is only when Rodrigues too has been shorn of his certainties, his confidences, his battle-trained hard shell that he is able to hear what such a Christ has to say. It is a message his old self would have regarded as blasphemous. Now he can receive it as a word of life.

"It is to be trampled on by you that I am here." Some people find a God who can say that, live that, deeply shocking. How can a God who allows himself to be trampled on be God at all? Is it not the very essence of God to be worshipped, held in great esteem, magnified? What would one think of a king who allowed his subjects to walk all over him — and if not a king, then a *god*? You might find it helpful here to look at your own images of God, and more particularly the power/humility poles in those images. Do you worship a God whose major, perhaps exclusive, characteristic is his (or her) majesty, conceived in a more or less medieval courtly mode? Or do you worship a God whose glory lies in her readiness to be trampled?

One way to approach this is to re-enact in your imagination the scene from *Silence*, with you as Rodrigues. . . . Take it slowly and allow yourself to become aware of all your feelings as you contemplate grinding your heel in the face of the Christ who is inviting you to trample him. . . . Another approach, through the imagination and memory, is to recall an occasion in which you saw someone being utterly humiliated. Recreate that scene in your imagination and then substitute Christ for the one who was humiliated. . . . Look carefully at your feelings . . . .

Most people who do this exercise are surprised by their own anger at seeing Christ thus trampled, either literally or metaphorically. Very few people, in my experience, can bring themselves to allow their feet to touch the icon, preferring, if they can stand the imaginative pressure that long, to see Christian prisoners tortured: or they beg the guards to execute them . . . .

For we find the notion of a truly humble Saviour either incredible; or revolting; or deeply threatening. There are many reasons for that, one of the simplest being that we have never taken seriously Paul's analogy with slavery: ". . . Yet he did not think to snatch at equality with God, but made himself nothing, assuming the nature of a slave. Bearing the human likeness, revealed in human shape, he humbled himself, and in obedience accepted even death – death on a cross." There are three ideas there that would have seemed at least as scandalous to a good Pharisee as Endo's scene seems to us. The idea of a God as slave – and notice how strongly Paul puts it: assuming the nature of a slave (not "appearing like a slave" or "pretending to be a slave"). Such an idea was not only paradox: it was deeply offensive. For though slaves were not taken to be an inferior species or a lower moral order, the very status of slave was a mark of God's great displeasure. A God who assumed *that* nature simply was not to be taken seriously.

But Paul goes on, heaping scandal on contradiction. He emphasizes, by repeating it twice, the humanity of Christ. Although divine, he bore the likeness, the shape of humanity. To Greek and Jew alike, this is religious language gone wild. Even Moses could not look upon God, catching a glimpse only of his back. To see God was, for any human, to court instant death. Yet, says Paul, this same God actually assumed human form . . . Blasphemous nonsense!

Death on a cross — for Greeks and Romans the lowest, most despicable form of execution, reserved for criminals of the most dangerous or despicable variety. For Jews a formal declaration of curse; that is, a proclamation of final, irreparable separation from God. How could a God be thus cursed? It was not just nonsense: it was deeply repugnant nonsense.

It is not only, however, that we have lost the cognitive impact of Paul's Gospel. It is rather, I suspect, that we do not want, at bottom, a God who thus turns everything upside down. We prefer a super-powered God who manipulates us and our history from a safe distance, guaranteeing us victory, prosperity and success. Now that, we think, really is a God worth worshipping. We symbolize that by maintaining a strictly hierarchical priesthood, even, notice, clothing our bishops (with little dissent from them) in the purple of imperial power. If those who act as intermediaries or representatives can lay claim — in however vestigial a form — to that degree of power, let us put them, and keep them, at the head of the army of God. Maybe some of their power will rub off on us.

By contrast a God who demeans himself to a lesser status than even we ourselves, and then confounds confusion by asking to be walked all over, who wants a God like that? What, we ask, is the point of a God who shares our lot, or worse than our lot, when what we want is a God who will transform our lot?

And there is the paradox — and it is a paradox so deep and so rich that it constantly slips out of our grasp. For it is precisely in sharing our lot that Christ transforms it. Weakness, vulnerability, poverty, insignificance, nothingness become not characteristics to be shunned or escaped or struggled against. They become the stuff of eternal life, a quality of life, that is, which is consistent with the Kingdom of God. Conversely power, authority, wealth, importance, respectability and fame are declared to be suspect, dangerous, unlikely to lead us towards the Kingdom. What men of the world – a revealing phrase – regard as desirable is declared by Christ to be undesirable. What men of the world seek to avoid and resist is declared to be where we are likely to stumble across the signs of the Kingdom.

May I challenge you to put that to the test of your own experience? Ask yourself where you have glimpsed a quality of life that the Bible calls eternal? Or, better, where in your own experience have you been most conscious of the Christ in your inner self? In moments of triumph, success, worldly acclamation? Or in moments of fear, failure and lostness? Spend a little time recalling particular times at each end of the spectrum of success. . . . Re-enter the scene and recapture how you felt. . . . Now ask yourself: where was Christ in that event? how did I relate to him at the time? . . . I do not want to dogmatize: people's experiences are different, fascinating in their diversity. All I can say is that in my own experience, and in that of many people I know well, it is those times of weakness, failure and lostness that seem the richest in retrospect – just as it is in the unimportant, insignificant and unsuccessful people that I most vividly apprehend the love of Christ in the world. Princes of Church and State – or, for that matter, of industry, sport or media – may have a role to play. We do not need to judge that. But the Christ who breaks his silence with most of us, I suspect, is the Christ who knows the taste of the mud of life.

Seen from this perspective, St Paul's paradoxical claim – poor ourselves, we bring wealth to many – becomes not only intelligible but entirely natural. St Paul was constantly aware of his poverty, his weakness — and if he was ever in danger of forgetting it, it seems he had his critics, especially at Corinth, who were only too happy to remind him of it. It is out of this weakness that he can proclaim the richness of the graciousness of God. He can, as it were, validate and even dignify weakness, vulnerability and failure as the stuff with which God can work. And that is the greatest richness he could offer anyone. For what can surpass the grace of God in the life of anyone who has been touched by it?

There is one final point to be made. "Poor ourselves, we bring wealth *to many*." Not to all; not even to anyone who wants it. For not everyone can receive the richness of the grace of God from those who allow themselves to be walked all over. Like Naaman, we expect some mighty work or wonder from an eminent figure. To find the grace of God in the trivial, the ordinary or the unimportant is alien to us. And so we miss it. Paradox upon paradox, then. The power of God is mediated through weakness; and received in weakness. It took, after all, a peasant girl to see the truth:

> the arrogant of heart and mind he has put to rout,
> he has brought monarchs from their thrones,
>   but the humble have been lifted high.

Even Rodrigues found that — in the end.

Summary of Exercises

1. Look at your images of God. Are they of a Baron God? Or a trampled icon?

2. Recall seeing someone humiliated. Substitute Christ for that someone. . . .

3. Where have you been most conscious of the Christ in your inner self? (p. 110)

8.

Penniless, We Own The World

It is a sad day when a normally bouncy, frisky dog keeps to its basket or kennel. Perhaps it will come out for a minute or two, but, hanging its head and with tail down, it returns to its sleeping place. That is often the sign of serious illness or even the approach of death. Like dogs, very many other animals, humans included, show the same desire to return to somewhere they feel completely safe whenever they are hurt or sick. I know myself the sense of relief and fittingness with which I have shut my bedroom door and flopped on to my bed, after a long journey home with some violent, unidentified sickness.

It is akin to a return to the womb: indeed, sick animals or badly hurt people – whether physically hurt or emotionally hurt – often adopt a foetal position as they nurse their pain. They may even want the conditions of the womb recreated – darkness (so we draw the curtains); warmth (fill a hot-water bottle); constriction (tuck up the bedclothes tight); quiet (turn off that distant radio). They want to return to the womb because that is where they felt totally safe, and in their present distress, they need to feel safe again.

If this need to feel safe is demonstrated most overtly at times of great physical or emotional trauma, it is a constant feature of our inner landscape. It is indeed one of the most basic needs we have. Without it we can never develop into fully free individuals, secure in our own identity, at ease with ourselves, free enough to open ourselves to others. It is such a basic need that we *will* meet it, or strive to do so, by fair means or foul, even if we never become fully conscious that the need is unmet. Without really knowing what we are doing, we will look for substitute forms of security.

And that is something at which we are expert. Our problem is that these substitutes can deliver only a tiny fraction of the security we crave. Realizing, again often unconsciously, that we are not getting out all we need, we put more and more into the substitute. And that can only bring disappointment and pain, both to us and, very often, to the substitute.

We can see this happening in many man/woman relationships. One of the basic drives that powers those relationships, perhaps more for the man than for the woman, is a desperate need – and I use that adjective carefully – for the security that has so far been denied. He invests more and more of himself in her, searching for something that, however hard she tries, she can give only in the faintest outline. Sensing that she can give him a little, he assumes that if he puts yet more into the relationship, she will be able to satisfy that huge hunger. He makes impossible demands on her – and becomes hurt or angry when she cannot meet them. Maybe he despairs of her and goes elsewhere in search of a security no woman can give him. One broken relationship follows another . . . .

It is not, of course, only in "romantic" relationships that this process is at work. The role of the woman in the scenario above may be played by an institution – a firm, a school, a political party or, supremely, the Church. It is not entirely coincidental that the Church is often referred to as feminine: "she" is the Bride of Christ. She also acquires the same set of demands as the woman. Surely she can offer the security, the acceptance, the basis for self-identity that romantic relationships finally fail to deliver? Like romantic relationships, she can – but only up to a point.

And there's the rub. So much more is asked of her than she can in fact make good, but because she can offer something, more and more is put into the relationship in the hope that more can be squeezed out. Loyalty to "the Church" becomes the touchstone not only of faith but of life itself. More tragically than ever, the Church as the pilgrim (and wayward) people of God is often relegated to a subordinate position, and this particular denomination or parish or, most destructive of all, this particular building, becomes the recipient of all my longings for a safe haven in which my very essence can be affirmed and made real. So don't meddle with it! If you start changing things about or even dare to threaten its closure in the interests of "efficiency" or "economy" or "good stewardship", watch out. I will fight with every claw at my disposal because you are assaulting me at my most vulnerable point. I cannot stand that kind of pain: resistance and aggression are my only defence. You will dismiss me as conservative, cantankerous, foolish, neurotic — but only because you do not understand the depth of my need and the sharpness of my pain. You think I am defending an out-dated building; actually I am defending something that I want to function as a womb. And my pain is the worse because my chosen womb-substitute seems unable or unwilling to function very effectively. If only you would leave it alone, perhaps it would function better . . . .

At a more insidious level we may not look directly to a building or even an institution for security: we may look rather at the *raison d'être*, the ideas behind the institution — the "values" of a school; the "quality of care" of a hospital; the *esprit de corps* of a regiment; the theology of a church. *Odium theologicum* is a patholigical reality that is terrifying in its inversion of all the Christian faith claims to be about. And if we ask why challenge to settled theological ideas unleashes so much hatred, violence and ugliness, the answer I believe lies precisely in the same area. Deprived of the deepest emotional security and unable perhaps to discover it in sexual relationships or anywhere else, we — and this is particularly true of our over-intellectualized, hypercerebral western Christianity — look for it in the dogmatic certainties of our faith. In an outer world so patently insecure, uncontrollable and constantly changing; and in an inner world in which our identity cannot be affirmed by the love of another, we know not who we are. We can define ourselves and our world only by reference to "eternal verities" that need elements of mystery and mysticism to satisfy the unfathomable depths of our craving. Expose those "verities" to criticism; or chip away at the mystery; or wonder aloud at the compensatory nature of the mysticism, and you lay the axe to the roots of my self-hood. My reaction may indeed look like "odium": it is in reality a primal cry to be spared an unendurable hurt.

We need not limit the discussion to so churchy an example. For the commonest form of substitute security is wealth — straight, unadorned lucre. A number of psychological studies of super-rich *nouveaux riches* have shown that a recurrent feature of their make-up is a desire for security at a far deeper level than keeping the bank manager at bay. What they are looking for is identity, to know who they are — and they are in doubt about that because they lack the inmost security that affirms their identity. Wealth and its trappings, they imagine (again often only half-consciously), will fill the hole at the centre of their being. Certainly it will give them outer security: they will never go hungry or naked. They expect it, too, to bestow an inner rootedness, an at-one-ness with themselves. Again, it is a cruel treadmill. Wealth, like romance or institutional loyalty or dogma, can help a little. Even at the deeper level, it can make a marginal contribution: "If I had more, I would feel even better." So I work harder, perhaps less scrupulously, in the hope that more money will bring greater security. For a time, it may seem that it does. I cannot, however, live on the modest return of security my ever greater wealth gives me. So I look elsewhere — to women, perhaps, or drugs or politics. Or religion.

So far I have described this lust for security purely in individual terms. That is the most basic level at which each of us experiences it. It comes, however, in other forms. Although the origins and symptoms may be different in important respects, it is clear that institutions, societies and particularly nation-states lust for security in much the same way as do individuals. The same tragic treadmill is discernible. How else explain the madness of the arms race? Yes, a nuclear balance and mutually assured destruction may indeed offer a form of security. But the balance must be tipped ever so slightly in our direction to give us that vital bit of extra security. Which it may . . . for a time . . . until they do the same. . . . What began as a promise that would meet our deepest need in global politics becomes a monster that delivers the reverse of security. The parallel with romantic love is close. . . .

What is common to all the reactions I have described is the assumption that security lies in having — having an affair; having a creed; having money; having power; having weapons; having more, irrespective of what. That is very understandable. If our deepest experience is that of denial — denial, that is, of the security we crave so badly — it is almost inevitable that we shall seek to compensate for that denial by acquisition. I wonder if that is your experience, too? Maybe it would be helpful, before we go any further in exploring this paradox, if you were to take a few minutes (and you may want to come back to this several times) to do two things, neither of them simple. The first is to acknowledge your own need for security: and the second is to look at the ways in which you do in fact meet that need. Let's look at those in order.

The exercise takes us back to the first few paragraphs of this chapter, but first we need to make explicit a distinction that there remained implicit — that between comfort and security. Imagine you have just been given some terrible news, news that affects you personally and immediately. Perhaps – and this would be better – you can remember such an event? First, watch what you do. Where do you go? Where do you wish to be? Whom do you want to talk to? – if you want to talk at all. In other words, in a moment of crisis, of trauma, where do you look for comfort? Second, ask yourself what kind of comfort you expect/desire/need to receive.

Have a closer look at yourself in this imagined (or re-called) situation – and see whether it reveals anything about what seems finally important to you when a major plank in your life crumbles. Then look critically at what it was that you *imagined* had been the occasion of this trauma. The death of a loved one? The collapse of a relationship? News of a far-advanced cancer? Your choice of trauma with which to inflict yourself in imagination may well show you where at least one source of your security currently lies. . . . It might be a good idea to ask yourself about the kind of security it does in fact offer – and the kind of demands you are actually making of it.

This is emphatically not an invitation to pass judgement on yourself: that will be very unhelpful. It is to encourage you to look at your own sources of security and check that you are not putting yourself and others on the destructive treadmill I have described earlier. You may well be surprised at how remarkably liberating facing the need for security and viewing the relationship (whether it be with an individual or an institution or a set of ideas) from that perspective can be. Our needs do not necessarily change: but our understanding of how we are trying to meet them through other people enables us to ask of our relationships only what it is within their capacity to deliver.

When we do the opposite – that is, ask more of our relationships than is reasonable – we are in danger of literally worshipping false gods. For we are ascribing worth, ultimate worth, to people or structures that, however good they may be, are certainly not ultimately worthy. Only God can sustain that claim. Only he liberates and redeems on a scale and at a level that offers us the security we try to squeeze out of the substitutes — idolatrous substitutes, as it now turns out — we were looking at earlier. It is because he has overcome all the powers of evil and diminishment through the Cross and resurrection of Christ that we can speak of his liberation of the whole cosmos. That does not guarantee us a painless, trouble-free or successful journey through our bit of the cosmos; but it does mean that however grave the pain, trouble or failure we experience in that journey, those hurts do not define the end of the journey. Let me illustrate with a true story.

A young mother was awoken one night by a suspicious noise. She woke her husband, who went into the garden to investigate. He was grabbed by thieves, severely beaten up and tied. The thieves then broke into the house. As the mother and her two small children were herded into the sitting room, she realized that the thieves were so high on drugs that they were jumpy, violent and scarcely knew what they were doing. The children intuited the degree of danger they were in. The mother tried to comfort them. ". . . . But they will kill us . . .", the seven-year-old sobbed. Retelling the story later, the mother said: "At that point, I knew I had to be honest — honest with Jamey and honest with myself. To my own surprise, I heard myself say: 'That's possible. But even if they do, it really doesn't matter . . .' And I meant that so deeply that fear vanished and the children became quite calm and composed." In a moment of crisis, she discovered a cosmic security that enabled her to face the brutal murder of her family.

Maybe we can now see more clearly the scale of Paul's paradox: Penniless ourselves, we own the whole world. Paul had no idolatrous securities — not wealth nor friends nor institutions nor dogmas. His one security was the

Gospel of Christ crucified and raised from the dead — and, as he emphasized to the Ephesians and the Colossians, that was enough to ensure that the powers of darkness would not finally triumph. And if that is so, we need fear nothing. We have a truer security than even ownership of the whole world could secure for us.

Again, we need to test that against our own experience. We've tried to look at some of our false securities: now let's look at cosmic security. Recall your worst fear; the one thing in life that makes you sweat with fear, gives you nightmares, leaves you anxious and emotionally wrung-out. Enter that fear so that it becomes alive, real. Then share it with Christ. Describe it to him. Tell him how you feel; why you feel it. . . . And see what he has to say about it.

Summary of Exercises

1. Look at your own need for security . . . (pp. 117–18)

2. Look at where you do actually find security . . . (p. 118)

3. Share your worst fears of insecurity with Christ.

9.

Epilogue

The point of this book is to encourage you to look for — and expect to find — the essence of the resurrection in daily life. I have suggested that one way of doing that (not, of course, the only way) is by reflecting on your own story in the light of Paul's story. That makes your own story central to your capacity and readiness to enter into the living kernel of the Gospel of God. Your story, then, demands to be taken seriously.

How, though, to "get hold of" your story? For most people, most of the time, life is lived as a series of discrete events, one following the other unassimilated, undifferentiated. And the more pressured the life we lead, the less the space we have for assimilation and differentiation. Consider, by contrast, the habit of one of the greatest creative geniuses of our day. After a major concert when he has explored the farthest reaches of his own humanity, Yehudi Menuhin usually stays in bed for a day, fasting. He needs that time of recollection, of inner settling, to ensure that next time he performs the same works his understanding and reinterpretations of them will advance: to be certain, that is, that he does not go stale. Sure, we are not virtuosi and we cannot "afford" a day in bed after a particularly intense experience. By refusing to recognize the need to gather our story, however, we run the risk of allowing our inward creativity to go stale.

Apart from allowing space, what else can be done to enable us to reflect on our story? There are a variety of techniques on offer: journalling, the periodic writing of a faith history, the disciplined reflection on the interaction of inner and outer lives by means of a formal array of questions or through the gentle probing of a skilled spiritual director. Perhaps such a list sounds daunting or over-professional or over-technical, more suited to the cloister than to the kitchen sink. That would be a pity, because in fact none of these techniques are so high-powered or demanding that they are beyond the reach of anyone who has read thus far. There is, however, a less formal way of being in touch with our own story, one that I personally have long found helpful.

It starts with two important assumptions: first, that there is something releasing and yet focusing about story-*telling*. Laying it out in words, in a coherent set of observations, has its own discipline and its own power. Second, story is a communal activity. Story is to be shared. Now certainly our own story, with its admissions of failure, sin and refusals to come alive, cannot and should not be shared with every Tom, Dick and Harriet. With people we trust; whose loving friendship we can take for granted; whose own story, for good and ill, we can encounter, we may well find the courage to be free. And, if we are lucky, we shall find that they can help us understand our story, both by laying it alongside their own, by keeping it perhaps in a healthier perspective than we can, and therefore helping us to relate it more creatively to biblical material, the relevance of which may have escaped us.

A story-sharing group which meets regularly rather than frequently is the forum in which this exchange can take place. It will take place, however, only if there is a high degree of mutual trust, affection and acceptance within the group. To a limited extent that can be created by a good group leader, and to a larger extent it can be nourished and fostered by the group as a whole. In my experience, however (and I have no means of knowing how general this may be), the greatest nourishment comes from the stories themselves.

Another important component seems to be the sharing of celebration – which may be something as homely as a shared meal served with care and generosity, or as deeply symbolic as a Eucharist planned and executed by the group as a whole.

Such a group may or may not be for you. Some people find it hard to speak their inmost thoughts, fears and failings, even to a few supportive friends (though, like fighting, they often find it only needs a start). For them a variant of what Father Richard Buck calls a "ponder-paper" may be appropriate. I have adapted one such paper from Father Buck at the end of this book. If this is your way to your own story, you may wish to develop your own ponderpapers as you become aware of the parts of your story that are harder to bring into focus.

So much for story, your story. How to relate it to Paul's astonishing discovery that dying we are yet alive? There can be no one answer to that, for resurrection appears in different guises. Resurrection is the Spirit at work. It is therefore invisible, unpredictable, surprising, paradoxical, waiting to be stumbled over on the map of life. One relatively simple starting point – and it is only a starting point; the beginning of an agenda not the agenda itself – is to look for whatever it is that makes you more you, more wholly in touch with what you are at your deepest part. One sign of that will be joy, by which I don't mean only happiness or laughter or fun (though at times they will come, too). By joy I mean a sense of wholeness, of integration, of inner truth and trust that so enhances the quality of life that we glimpse what is meant by life eternal.

That can come as a shock. I suspect it often does. For if we are honest we may find that what brings joy is not the "holy" things we thought we ought to find – liturgy, sacrament, fellowship, Bible reading, prayer, contemplation. It may be something quite different – hoeing a row of beans, or Johnny Dankworth, or rigging singing in the wind of an anchorage, or laughter round a dinner table, or yielding to a lover's embrace. If that is where resurrection life is for you, find the courage to honour it — en-joy it. Shout hosannas for that row of beans, that embrace.

Then comes the rest of the agenda. If I know where there is death in my life and I know now where there is life, what is God doing in me with those great themes? There, at that point, God is at work. . . . How now do I honour both the death and the life? That question seems to me to be at the heart of the spiritual journey.

It is at the heart of that journey, not only for us as individuals (though it is often easier to see at the individual level), but also for our institutions, both secular and sacred. We should never forget that Paul writes in the first person plural. Although the experience of rejection, humiliation and frustration had been supremely, perhaps in its bitterest moments exclusively, his alone, the faith he proclaims is of life for the community — we live; we own the world; we have cause for joy. . . . The experience Paul describes *can* be a communal one, as I illustrated in some of the stories in this book. Supremely it *can* be the experience of the Church. In South Africa, South Korea, Central America, Russia, Brazil, the evidence is there. But it is evidence from people who have looked death in the face. Perhaps the final paradox is that it is only when our churches are brought to that brink that we shall discover institutional life. . . . In the meantime we would be as foolish to ignore the experience of those who are discovering it, day by suffering day, as we would be to ignore the experiences of Paul himself.

Milestones

These questions are neither a parlour game nor an invitation to self-flagellation. They are designed to help you discover your story, and reflect on God's loving purpose for you in the past and the future.

1. If I break my life into natural segments – childhood, adolescence, early adulthood, early years of marriage, etc. – can I see any pattern, or only confusion and randomness?

   Are there any common elements in those periods?
   Which gave me the greatest sense of purpose and inner tranquillity?
   Which was the most difficult, and why?
   In which did I make the most enduring friendships?
   Why have friendships made in other periods lapsed?
   Which figures in each period do I still admire – and why?
   Which figures from each period do I still remember with distaste – and why?
   How would each – those I admired and those I disliked – react to me if they met me today?

2. What major decisions have I made that explain where I am today?

How did I make those decisions? Whom did I talk to about them? Why?

Would I make the same decisions now? In the same way?

If not, how do I react to the thought that I may have made mistakes?

What major decisions lie ahead? How am I preparing for them?

3. Where would I like to be, in the best of all possible worlds, in five years' time?

What would my friends say of that ambition? What would Christ say?

What am I going to do about it?

If I had been asked the same four questions five years ago, what would I have said? How does that sound now?

4. What would I describe as peak-experiences — in my life? in the last two years? this month?

How did I react to those peak experiences?

5. What would I describe as trough-experiences — in my life? in the last two years? this month?

How did I react to those trough experiences? Did I discern God in either peak or trough? How?

6. How far is my sense of God dominated by an individualized spirituality?

Where do I see/seek/find God in institutions?

7. What would I die for?

8. Whom would I live for?

9. Where do I most feel me?

   Where am I most conscious of God as loving companion?

10. Of what am I afraid?

    What is the ground of that fear?

11. Which of the Pauline paradoxes do I most easily identify with? Why?